FAME ON YOU

50 SHAMELESS WAYS TO MAKE YOU FAMOUS

A Satirical Memoir of Sorts

John D. Thompson, c, 2015

NO TABLE OF CONTENTS AND NO PAGE NUMBERS!

I had to make my way through this mess,

and so can you!

In Loving Memory of Kent Vlautin

Author's Note

It behooves me to preface this book
by making one point clear.

This isn't a memoir, at least in the purest sense.
At times, this book may read like a memoir.

But remember.
This is not pure memoir.
It may be pure something,
but not a memoir.

In fact, I am starting
a new literary genre:
loutrageous-lit,reading that is lousy
and outrageous!

And this book is **not** for the faint-hearted.
It is not for the hearted period.
Furormore, I am dedicating these pages
to the heartless... and their shameless pursuit of fame.

Reader discretion is advised.

Readership of this loutrageous lit is ill-advised.

All Typographical Errors Are Like Hotel Guests of This Book,
They are INN-tentional.

ISBN: 0972071792
LIBRARY OF CONGRESS CONTROL NUMBER: 2015918491

FAME ON YOU: 50 Shameless Ways to Make You Famous
Copyright, 2015, John D. Thompson

Manufactured in the United States of America

Palindrome Publishing of Iowa

PROLOGUE

I want to begin with a line or two about copyright infringement. It involves tramps, thieveries, and gypsies all wheeling around for show in what appears to be the merchandising of medicinal wares by an elderly man who should be off that wagon in more ways than one. But the lines aren't my own and they're not absolutely true about my life. They would be pilfered from a Cher song (love her) circa early 1970s. You know the one, and I am not talking about the song where she is bred in half! But, honest to God, like the lyrics themselves, my mom was 16 and my dad 21 when they hitched their wagon to my eventual star. At any rate, you have to look for the figurative bull behind the matador's cloak to see their relevance. Any lawyers yet? Rainmakers? Can anyone around here drum up a little bottle o' business? No? My point is this…

The Golden Rule to Fame is

STEAL EVERYTHING

Theft for your betterment is so crucial that it needs to be spotlighted here instead of embedded in the 50 chapters ahead of you, passages to your claim to fame, as it were. Think of this kind of theft as a patch-quilt project…take a little here…take a little there…and wa-la! You're a creative, inventive individual whose *famometer** is on fire. Fever. Add *–or* to *fever* in the right place, and you have *forever*.

And before we go any further, let me be totally honest about the purpose of this book: Me and the pathetic pursuit of fame while teaching high school in the middle of a corn field. I am not kidding. I could literally stop writing this instant, walk outside, and either start detasseling or be run over by a harvest combine just feet away from this laptop, depending on the season or reason. My God, what was that, that just went past my winda? I mean, window? The top of its head looked like a petrified tumbleweed you could hang Christmas ornaments on? Hand me my deer rifle, Buford!

Trust me, this place puts the *ache* in acreage. But dreams and their pursuits can begin anywhere…even somewhere over the pig trough. I can't tell you how many times I have looked out the glass of this portable, pseudo-classroom and prayed for my time with a tornado. But this place has made me what I am today—

petty, bilious, and looking for fame in all the wrong places. And I hope this book does for me what a rainbow did for Dorothy.

famometer-register to measure fame based on applause, approval, and public appetite for you.

PRE-TEST: What's Your FIQ?

aka FAME FOR DUMMIES

A lot of stupid human beings are famous. Tim Tebow for one. Tim Tebow for another. My point is, Do not be intimidated by lack of **FIQ**—your Fame Intelligence Quotient—or FAME SMARTS as I like to put it. The fact that you're bellying up to this book is a clear indicator that you want to do something about your FIQ. And if someone ever rides you about your lack of fame sense, just sport a finger of choice and say "FIQ" to their critical crassness. They will get the picture and see the light in the same gesture.

Here are a few questions to assess your FAME INTELLIGENCE QUOTIENT?

1) With what hand do you shield your face from the shutter-bug paparazzi?

ANSWER: Neither!

Is there any reason for further testing? If you can't tell which came first, the Madonna or the Wanna, you've got a lot of page turning to do or the Lady GaGa in you might just turn into the Lady GagGag!

Note to the Fame Incompetent:

An *FIQ Quiz* threads the book. Answers in the Appendicitis.

Cheat if you have to.

PREFACE: A RULE BEFORE THE RULES:

CRUELTY WORKS

If honesty is the best policy,
cruelty is the underwriter of the policy.
Beat me up emotionally.
You know how to do it!
When choosing a, for lack of better terminology—friend,
I search for the human being who can give me the worst possible time,
and that's when yours falsely makes my move.

Have you ever noticed that whether
on vacation or enjoying some leisurely moment
that cruelty is abruptly absent?

That is because cruelty is back on your farm of furor—
working.
And that's quite a back forty it must tend to.

Meanness is for the moment; cruelty is constant.
This is an important distinction aboard the rollercoaster ride of fame.
Case in point,
Natalie Wood may have thought she was on a pleasure cruise
during that holiday sail, Thanksgiving 1981;
but also on board was Captain Cruelty.
Unfortunately for her,
Thanksgiving became Planksgiving—
springing her a seawater awakening of ruthless truth.

Enjoy fame while you can,
because cruelty and its sidekicks
of envy and jealousy are working against you 24/7.

RULE OF FAME # 1: INSIST ON IT

Before we further this fame fiasco, it is imperative that you know what the word *imperative* means. It is a command, a necessity, the ultimate to-do word whether you do it, or you boss someone else around enough, so they do it for you.

The youngest of four children, I grew up in a household of imperatives, in which everyone (dad and we kids) spoke to our poor mom in, what I call *command communication*. You know, we'd tell her what to do. I myself would command her around like a drill sergeant to the freshly enlisted. This was no home to be the inspiration for shows like *The Waltons* or *Little House on the Prairie*. This was more like *Big Barracks on the Prairie* or *The Wallbangers*.

My father lived to make money, and he threw it around like ticker-tape at a World Series Parade. Just about every sentence out of his mouth began with an active-voice verb: a do-or-die threat, or demand. He was a work-a-holic, even at home. I can still see it today—Dad on the couch or folks' bed and puffing away at cigarette 6,000 for the day, his white work socks yellow with tar and nicotine, while he was yelling at some poor cattle distributor to make him richer. He made the Marlboro Man look like Nancy Reagan's *Just Say No* campaign. He was either smoking or smoking mad at someone or both. Whenever he spoke my name, *John*, it was immediately followed by *Goddamnya'*. For years, I thought this was my middle name. John Goddamnya' Thompson.

But I'll say one thing about Stiff Cliff (his first name was Clifford, which he hated), he taught us kids how to get what we wanted, and we siblings first and foremost took it out on dear ol' Mom.

"Make me biscuits and gravy," my older brother would tell her at breakfast.

"Make us some French toast," my sisters would collectively call.

"Make me famous," I insisted. This woman knew I was dead-eye serious. I'd say it to her while staring at that piece of forehead between her eyebrows, known as the **glabella**. Then, I would ignore her until it was the next time to feed me. Why, I am told the first word I ever spoke was *Beware!* It, too, is an imperative if you think about it.

Do.

RULE OF FAME # 2: FORGET YOUR ROOTS

Whether it's your place of birth, childhood hometown, or graying hair follicles— you have got to forget your roots. The famous need their roots like Helen Keller needs a set of state-of-the-art BEATS headphones. (I swear that is the first and last Helen Keller joke.) To the renowned, hometowns are for Hall of Fame inductions and parades to grand marshal. Aside from these occasions, get out and stay out of town. "There is no place like home" does not apply to the media magnificent. "There is no place like Hollywood."

Burn every bridge you can like an arsonist covered in turpentine about to enter a tanning booth. You gave your family and hometown the privilege of knowing you as a child prodigy trapped in a hell-hole. Now, it is time to forget them and move forward. They will only want you for photo ops and residual checks, anyway. Tell them to do their own damn chores. Your chore was to put up with them all those years while you were waiting to get famous. Let them sweat it out. You've got a cucumber facial and a foundation make-up call for which to be fashionably late.

Remember. Forget your roots. They will do nothing for you unless you're Arthur Haley, LeVar Burton, or Leslie Uggams. Your point of origin is pointless. Conk yourself over the head with a lead frying pan and pray for amnesia if you have to. The only time to remember your roots is when the flickers of fame begin to dwindle and dowse in your waning years and not even plastic surgery or a construction firm can save your face from dragging on like a 6-hour PBS special. Then, write a histrionic, hysterical memoir exposing your hometown and family for the sitcom-cesspools of scandals they are, and don't worry about how much of it is the truth. Do you see the word *ruthless* in *truthless*?

Old Blue Eyes, Frank Sinatra…his daughter, Nancy, said it best… almost. Them boots are made for walkin'…and those roots were made for walking over any past existence that does directly correlate or contribute to your fame.

RULE OF FAME # 3: OUTSHINE YOUR SIBLINGS

If charity begins at home, so does fame. Do you see the root of **fame** in **family**? Believe me, it's in there. You've got to be better than your brothers and sisters, or your chances for celebrity in this slippery world are as slim as a dime on a diet. For me, this was *easy-peasy*. Outshining my siblings was a piece of pastry, cake on a platter. All three of them are as dull as a lead landscape on a gray harbor. I had to keep my poor mother entertained constantly, or I swear she was going to go all cabin fever on us and spray bullets through the living room like a pez dispenser. My siblings were so lackluster, every time they aligned, I thought I was a contestant on *Let's Make a Deal*…Door # 1, Door #2, Door #3. And no matter what dumb door I picked, it was always a consolation prize on the other sorry side, you know, a year's supply or Rice-a-Roni or Turtle Wax. *Wah! Wah! Wah!*

Even though they were taller and older than I, this kid always had the upper-hand on dim, dimmer and dimmest—another way I like to classify my siblings. I'll never forget it…Christmas, circa 1966. Kennedy should have still been in the White House. We children all slept in downstairs bedrooms while the folks and our beloved holiday tree about to be accoutered with Kris Kringle goodies all nestled above us on the ground floor. My older brother and two sisters got the collective idea to stuff me up through the heat ventilator to the first floor, so I could spy and tell them what they were receiving from the man with the bag. I can still feel their teamwork hands pushing my pampered tush up through that metal duct. I couldn't breathe; I couldn't see. Still, I was determined to outshine them on this, the darkest moment, literally and figuratively, of my early childhood.

I was wearing one of those one-piece sleep jumpers with snap fastens and sweating like a Watergate burglar testifying before Congress during the Nixon and Ford administrations. Soon, my chubby little face was pressed against the grill just outside the parents' dream domain. I felt like a waffle about to be served at IHOP. I don't know how I did it. Pure talent, most likely. But I managed to remove the grill, replace it, tip-toe in my jumper footies to the evergreen, take note, then dash downstairs to report to my anxious siblings. I lied through my scant teeth and reported a BB gun, typewriter, and full Barbie dream house, none of which was there. The next morning, when the disappointed duped complained to Mom and Dad, they were severely punished; and I spent Christmas morning playing with their stuff. Get the picture. Be the Kodak moment without any other kids. Be the brilliance before the bulb and leave the betrayed in the basement. It's better training for future fame than being a *Mouseketeer*!

RULE OF FAME # 4: BEFORE MONEY & FORTUNE…FAME!

The Irene Cara song, *Fame* (1980), I am sad to suggest, was wonderful but wrong. The famous do not necessarily have it all, and some of you will have to prioritize if not downright choose between or among money, fortune, and fame. In fact, if you're truly a pursuer of fame, the phrase should be fame, fortune, and money—not money, fortune, and fame. Besides, it's alphabetized that way. Fame must come first in your life—even before the chicken and the egg. Fame is *prima facie*, whatever that means, I just thought the book needed a Latin referent. If you don't believe me, check the civil rights archives. Abraham Lincoln, Rosa Parks, Gandhi, Mother Teresa—all of these eminent citizens of the nation and world had few pennies in their palms. And those poor Sesame Street muppets…if you think they ever received a nickel for tickling audiences' fancies, think again. PBS is cheaper than a newborn chick calling for its first worm.

Rock bands, comedians, poets, self-help authors who self-publish… all of these people start from nowhere and sometimes stay there…but their pursuit occasionally, occasionally brings them a flash of fame.

If you want to be famous, you may have to settle for what I call the "Afternoon Delight" syndrome, named after a one-wit wonder song circa 1976 by the Starland Vocal Band. Who? My point exactly. These losers even won the Grammy for Best New Artist. They were the Milli Vanilli of the Have-a-Nice-Day era. Name one member. Still, they knew fame. Fame soon forgot them.

But if you were alive and listening to the radio during our bicentennial year, I bet you remember the tune. Yes, the folks who crooned "Afternoon Delight" lasted about as long as a 3 PM quickie in a seedy motel on the dark side of town. It is a story, saga, and song that Bruce Springsteen forgot to record, *Harmony on the Edge of Obscurity*.

Why, I would throw my own mother in front of a fully-loaded double-decker tour bus jolt-trolling through the streets of London…for an hour of a fame massage from fickle fans…and then gladly wait in a soup line while I awaited federal sentencing. Fame is one part dedication, one part dreadication. Just as you have to kiss a stool full of toads to find your prince, you most likely will have to scrub a Taj Mahal full of stools to find fame, you toady. And there is only one way to turn that Fuller brush into your magical wand. Start scrubbing!

FIQ QUICK QUIZ # 1

(Answers in the back! Answers in the back!)

1. **What type of child has the most potential to ignite the fame flame?**

    A. The child who is kind and considerate toward others

    B. The child who is patient and forgiving as modeled by his forebearers

    C. The kid who treats his mom like the nickel-and-dime waitress she is

2. **While walking through the garden of fame's pursuits, forget your**

    A. fake ID

    B. the home and business address of the talent agent who messed with you

    C. roots

3. **It is important to outshine**

    A. Rudolph

    B. Shi# on shinola

    C. your siblings

4. **What comes before money and fortune?**

    A. a pre-ejaculator

    B. insider trading

    C. FAME! FAME! FAME!

RULE OF FAME #5: END YOUR SENTENCES WITH THE WORD, *BABY*

If it can work for Dick Vitale on every college basketball broadcast, baby, or Justin Bieber in any song he ever released, baby, it can work for you, baby. That's right, baby. Address anyone and anything in this world as baby, baby…and you've got it made, baby. Those of you who are as old as the trees that provided the paper that reamed this book—Remember Telly Savales as *Kojak*, baby? He solved crimes along the vicious streets of New York City while sucking a lollipop, baby. His bald head and those bald tootsie rolls soared through the Nielson ratings because he ended his sentences with baby, baby.

Back to Little Dickie Vitale, baby. The word *baby* is Vitale's children's vitamin, baby. It is the word of all words to cover his insecurity and inept vocabulary, baby—not to mention his lack of intuitive knowledge about roundball, baby. The one-word phrase *baby* especially comes in thumb-suck handy when the lights are beaming glints of superstar sweat off his caterpillar browline and those ESPN cameras are rolling during warm-ups, baby.

Can you say *clown* face, baby? NCAA Division I Basketball is his 3-ring circus, baby. And he's got the March Madness millions to prove it, baby. He's the slave master, I mean, ring master, baby. Who cares if he insults the athletic achievements of young men when he refers to them as *diaper dandies*, baby. Not mention the racially questionable imagery of Kunta Kinte being chained and dragged to a slave ship wearing a white wrap of Mandinkan man cloth around his pelvis, baby.

No, be hip like Dick, baby. Just keep rattling and prattling away, baby, and end those sport-side, court-side sentences with baby, baby. Soon, baby. It won't matter about the content or credibility of your broadcast or career for that matter, baby. You've got the boom market on *baby*, baby.

This youth-obsessed culture of ours will eat you up like Joey Chestnut on a Nathan's hot dog, baby. It's odd, baby. We're offended if folks address us as *you child*, baby. But, baby? It's a groupthink squirm of endearment, baby. It reeks with *I am young and cool, you are young and cool, we all are young and cool, baby.* And that's cool, baby! But what am I shaking my rattle for, baby? You cannot bottle fame, baby. You've got to baby fame, baby.

RULE OF FAME # 6: BABY, YOU'RE

A FIREWORK, BABY

If Katy Perry can make it, so can you, so can your used garbage bags, for that matter. But enough trash talk. No-talents are cluttering the Fame Plain, but that does not mean you cannot stake your acre of awesomeness. Look. If some over-the-hill pop diva in a pastel hooped mini-skirt red-riding her way through a forest of overgrown lollipop trees and wailing about California girls in Daisy Dukes, if someone like that can make it, you're on your way down Applause Avenue and turning right on Legendary Lane. California Girls? Hmmmph. More like California Great Aunt. She's so old that she still has threads on her left thigh from being in Betsy Ross' sewing circle. She's so old that she only thing she can do 3 times a night is use the bathroom. But I digress.

Evidently, all you need to be famous is cherry lipstick and make-up painted past the back of your ear lobes. Teenage dream is right. She hasn't been a teenager since the colonization of the country. The pilgrims have put a cave drawing of her on a cream bucket and reported her missing.

Katheryn Elizabeth (her real name) should be good at singing. After all, she was alive during the invention of sound.

But she keeps cranking out the 21st-century mindless, mind-boggling hits like a McDonald's French fryer during the lunch rush. And she makes me wish I were a firework. Because if I were, I'd pack an artillery of myself underneath the porch on the set of her next music video and pop her into the next Fourth of July. Boom, baby!

RULE OF FAME # 7: CONVINCE THE ELDERLY TO ADORE YOU

Living between funerals and waiting for God, the elderly population of this country, and the world for that matter, are longing for icons and acolytes to rock their remaining years. They are the "untouched" demographic of American culture, The Great Gray Hope for your fame aspirations. The elderly of our nation know all about the words *adore* and *adoration.* They became acutely acquainted with the adorable from being in those cute-as-a-bug's ear cherub's choirs exalting carols of the season for a century and appearing in Saturday afternoon Christmas pageants in and between both World Wars. But just as Santa was an illusion on ice, so was that plastic Baby Jesus in a manger of Sunday School craft yarn. They soon discovered the Son of God was nothing more than an abandoned Chatty Kathy doll with a buzz cut. And that the Angel of Glory was nothing more than an inverted snow cone with Barbie hair and crayons. A tragic realization among the tinsel and sugar cookies. After that, these fa-la-la's with false teeth have been longing to adore something, someone else. As the country duo The Judds once inquired, *Why Not Me*? Better yet, why not you? With Justin Bieber and cast of *The Big Bang Theory* having a stronghold with adolescents, especially females, you must look elsewhere for the age-group to give you monumental accolades and monetary ascenscion. Back to Bieber—He is a Girl Scout missing a few cookies, if you ask me. I wish the U. S. Postal Service, with its scant offices still surviving, would put his puppy mug on a federal stamp. Then millions of us would have a legitimate reason to drop him down a dark slot and send him to the unknown crevice-regions of the world. Now that would raise revenue for the financially-strapped post offices! Hey, I am just trying to do my part for this great country of ours!

Being ag-ed is being cag-ed. And if you set the old folks free, my friend, you'd be famous. Write something. Sing something. Do something that endears you to the boned and the brittled. Why I should be writing this sensational self-helper in **large print** just to attract the cataract'd and the crusty. The elderly are continuously being blitzkrieged by propaganda from Medicare, Medicaid, and infinite AARP commercials/mailings. It's like passing through a ticker-tape parade at the End-of-the-World Series. Trust me. The elderly are salivating between social security checks for a little pizzazz in their posterity.

Neil Young made a fortune by rhyming *Heart of Gold* with *Growing Old*. Does anyone know what rhymes with *Clandestine Swiss Bank Account?*

RULE OF FAME # 8: BE A REVOLVING DOOR, NOT AN EVOLVING BORE...

I have been in and out of the closet so much, I feel like a favorite suit. And, trust me, that suit has needed a much better dry cleaner through the years. My poignant point is this: Put the spin in your own life. What was once known as THE ROAD is now called THE CIRCUIT, and you better be one twister sister, my brother, if you intend to go the rounds.

Better to be a revolving door, than an evolving bore...or worse, what rhymes with *bore*, whor...? Keep your hands to yourself and keep people guessing. That's right. Walk around like you would do anybody; but, in reality, you wouldn't touch any of those cootie-comers with Paul Bunyan's pole vault. When addressing your public, be like a virgin, touched for the very first time...not for the very first time since 2nd period homeroom.

Human beings want what they cannot have. They crave it like a pregnant lady craves a Vlasic pickle in the same bowl with the Schwan's ice cream man wearing nothing but a popsicle stick and built like the truck in which he delivers the goods and treats, if you know what I mean. Let people envy you, but do not let them have you. Give it up and you go down...and not in a good way. Madonna recreates herself, so does a kindergartner playing in a sandbox. It is not hard to do. Spin and the world spins with you. Stagnate and you are moss on the pond just waiting for the local sewage department to do something about the complaints. If you can't stay fresh as a daisy, get out of the freaking field, Bambi. Fans have blades. That means your fans have blades, and they will mow right over you if you don't stay on the move, aloof, and in the unmowable groove.

FIQ QUICK QUIZ # 2

(Answers in the back! Answers in the back!)

5. **End all of your sentences with _____.**

    A. **death threats**

    B. **a beer burp from the lowest regions of your intestinal tract**

    C. **baby, baby**

6. **For Katy Perry, Thanksgiving is _____.**

    A. **just another holiday to let off her fireworks**

    B. **the day after Black Friday because she's calendar challenged**

    C. **a reunion/gathering at North America's first table for her and her pilgrim brothers and sisters**

7. **Convince the elderly to_____.**

A. **Ignore you**

B. **Abhor you**

C. **Adore you**

8. **Spin and_____.**

 A. **rinse**

 B. **after you sit on it**

 C. **and the world spins with you**

RULE OF FAME #9: PRETEND TO CARE

Have you ever noticed that the Queen of England waves to her subjects like she was opening a jar of jam? No, she isn't trying to "preserve" herself while out in public…pun intended. Rather, Her Royal Righteousness is pretending to care about her subjects and the whole fanfare. I mean, have you ever seen the hordes of roses they throw at that old bat? Does she ever stop the car or horses to pick up just one? Absolutely not! She is *above* what makes an Olympic figure-skating gold medalist or the latest women's Wimbledon champion bend over in front of ESPN cameras and scoop up a bouquet while exposing her backside to both hemispheres.

Lazy Liz simply refuses to stoop. And, best of all, she pretends to care. She wouldn't know a fellow Londoner from the surviving Boston Bomber. She couldn't tell a Rolling Stone from a Beatle! Why, I even heard that at Princess Di's funeral that confused ditz in a tiara mistook Sir Elton John tingling at the ivories for Dame Edna. Plausible.

And yet she rules the United Kingdom like inches rule a ruler. She can't tell Parliament from a peppermint, but the throne belongs to her tinsel tush. And she rules with a nodding nonchalance, like a horse on parade past Westminster Abbey, with blinders on. Her Majesty the Manikin has made a tea-and-crumpets career out of bluffing from Buckingham Palace while becoming the most gainfully unemployed person in human history. And you may be next!

Be as catatonic to those around you as a lifetime in-patient at the Bedlam Asylum in London. You may be able to draw flies with honey, but you gather fans through indifference. I do it all the time in the classroom where, at best, I am remotely interested in the cattle-call crowd-control state-mandated heathens that continuously occupy the desks before me—the Facebook freaks, the Twitter punks, the LinkedIn louts. They have numbed their minds with OMG, LOL nonsense so that their idea of a text in the classroom has nothing to do with books or a literary passage, but the latest good-for-nothing gossip that appears to make life bearable. I could not care less, but pretend to care—and care to pretend even more.

Our State Education Department wants us to teach to the Core. We should start by ripping out the cores of millions of hand-held packs of digital nicotine wreaking through the fingertips and veins of our electronic-tricked youth. But I digress. Mask your apathy for who or what is happening around you, and you will be dressed for dinner at the Welcome to the Hotel Hollywood, California.

PRETEND TO CARE PART II:

RIDE THE WAVE, THEN BREAK THE WAVE

I work in a wrestling factory. I swear—you cannot swing a dead cat without hitting a singlet wreaking of a bacteria colony. Is that a cauliflower growing in my ear? Each morning and night, I shower with Ajax and pray for cleansings. Actually, I teach high school, as mentioned—hello!—in central Iowa, the Wrestling Capitol of the World. Each winter, they role out the questionably smelling mats like a red carpet, kneel before the gods of Dan Gable, Cael Sanderson, and writer John Irving—and grapple away like it's nobody business.

I pretend to care. I have about as much respect for the sport as the Motown Romeo who jilted Aretha Franklin in the R & B song of the late 60s, *R-E-S-P-E-C-T*. In fact, if I were to write a song about our wrestling team, it would *I-N-S-P-E-C-T*. That's right, *Inspect!* Inspect academic eligibility, proper transfer papers, and—for God's sake—inspect what appears to be a bread-mold like fungus creeping in our locker rooms like the phantoms in Ghostbusters. Does anyone have a cake of Lava on 'em?

Recently, our wrestling team at won the traditional state wrestling team title at Wells Fargo in Des Moines. I am so jealous and envious that I am surprised these keys are not typing in green or a tasteful shade of jade. They have stolen my thunder overnight, but I am here to tell you, I will retort with a bolt of spring lightning!

That's right, I have a plan, Stan. But I need to be coy, Roy. Just listen to me. I am going to ride their wave of success and milk it like a prime, fat-teated FFA Jersey steer. I am going to wrest that crest until the tide subsides a-shore, then I am going to break and bust those Keebler elves like the little sand pebbles they are. Radical.

Don't you just love the word *Congratulations!?* You can say it with a snarl behind your teeth, and no one can tell how miserable you are about someone else's magnificence. As I write this entry, I am currently planning congratulatory cake parties for the four individual champions. They can choke on that cake, for all I care. There is no water fountain in my classroom, and I have purposely refused to learn the Heimlich. So snarf on that, you diet-deprived, rib-caged headline stealers! Come and get it.

RULE OF FAME # 10: DON'T LOVE PEOPLE BACK, GET PEOPLE BACK

People hate me, and I hate them back. I call this emotional equity, justice for the jugular. This may sound detrimental and downright unhealthy, but there are ways to channel hatred into cash and fame. Be someone people love to hate and watch cash and fame flow into your life like the Tigris-Euphrates. The more I hated Madonna, the more famous she became. The more I detested Woody Hayes as a child, the more games the Buckeyes won. The key to hate is treat it like a refundable bottle. Don't let it "bottle up" in you. Return the bottle for your due nickels. That's right. Make people who hate you pay and pay big. And don't collect too much hate, or it will clutter the rooms of your soul and make you into a hate hoarder. Messy. Recycle hate like the garbage it is. Just make sure people hear you clang those bottles when you throw them back in their deserved faces.

Get your five-cents worth out of people you wouldn't give two cents for!

This will come as a cattle-prod shock to most of you, but I once spoke to a therapist a time or two for a few problems encroaching my life like an offside defensive tackle or interior football buffoon of choice. And he said to me in one of those cathartic moments that Norman Rockwell forgot to brush and frame for the cover of the *Saturday Evening Post*.

He told me.

John, you've got to love people back. I thought I was going to lose my lunch on that couch. Luckily for me, it was 10 in the morning and I had skipped the Ebb McMuffin. Now, that's not a typo. An Ebb McMuffin is an Egg McMuffin that kicks back acid in your tummy after you've ingested while still in the drive-thru.

Real love hurts, people. So does revenge, but at least revenge is quick, one and done. Real love will occupy your life like those underemployed losers occupied Wall Street, and who needs that? Sharpen your savvy and hit people where they live. Your coccyx bone is really a Scorpion stinger that God didn't have time to develop on the Sixth Day before He took Sunday off. In the privacy of your own comfort zone, feel back there, and you will see what I mean. But remember—The stinger in you is the stinger in me.

Don't take my word for it, the Beatles devoted an entire song about it circa 1966, *Get Back!* At least, I think that's what they were harmonizing about. And didn't folk one-hit-wonder Shawn Colvin win a Grammy when *Sunny Came Home* with a mission. That was no Mormon mission, my mindless readers. She torched the place with a vengeance! Now, I am not talking bullets or bow and arrows. You don't need to be some whack job who wallpapers his room with *Field and Stream* or orders Gun Lovers pizza from the Hut. Kill 'em with kindness. Stew those juices like a tomato soup aficionado.

It's like a little lyric to a poem I once wrote, *Only if you leave me will I ever get you back / Nourish. Sustain. Sustain. Attack.*

To get yourself ahead you've got to get people back.

RULE OF FAME # 11: AMOUNT TO A HILL OF BEANS

I want you to rise and go to the kitchen, right here, right now. Once there, open the cupboard that stores dry beans or legumes. If your pantry or unit has neither—berries, grains, seeds, even dog-food pellets of some kind will do. Now cup a small quantity in your hands and walk to the table. Set the grains or beans down and make a little mound, heap, knoll, or hill with them. Then, sit yourself down and stare at the piddling hill, allow the mound to visually probe you as well, then ask yourself, *Am I worth more or at least tantamount in value to this hill of beans?* If *Of course, I am* does not reverberate from your voice box immediately, you've got some groundwork to do, my friend. Before you can ever climb Mt. Famous, first you must amount to a hill of beans.

Now as the Eagles once commanded a tramp they lorded over in a flatbed Ford–*Easy, easy.* You do not have be on an Olympic Team or *Jersey Shore* to amount to a hill of beans. But, by the way, if whatever you are staring at upon that table was purchased via food stamps, TRY HARDER! People will climb all over you like a concession worker selling sour grapes at a European soccer match after an overtime victory if you do not build that beanstalk, Jack.

That's right. Amount to a hill of beans. People respond to mounds. Just look at Major League pitching or Chippendale's dancing if you don't believe me.

RULE OF FAME # 12: KENNEL YOUR PAVLOVIAN DOGS

Despite popular theory or consensus belief, applause is not the most accurate index for fame, saliva is. Therefore, you've got to kennel those canine-like crowds that bark, hound, and, most of all, obey.

Never let the ordinary see you sweat, but make sure you see them spit!

It is all about stimulus-response, baby. So before you pack your pups into your pound of fame, you better have something for those chomps to salivate for. Ok, I ended a sentence with a preposition. Let me correct it. You better have something for those chomps to salivate for, stupid!

Fools drool!

If dog spit and a can of first-edition Alpo can make a no-talent like Pavlov famous in the science sect, imagine what throngs of thirsting fans can do for you? You all remember the story of Pavlov's dog and classical conditioning, don't you? Well, don't you? Check your Introduction to Psychology flash notes from college, people! Pavlov was the Russian dog that drooled even at the thought of something good—sort of like looking at Miley Cyrus on the *Bangerz* album before you break open the plastic wrap and, thus, breaking open your eardrums. You won't even need the plate of Kibble-n-Bits if you're good enough. America's Got Talent? Hmmph! America's Got Dog Food. Just make sure you've got the dish that most little doggies at the television and download window want. And the Labradors will retrieve and adore you, master.

Speaking of Russians and dogs, here's a Russian classically conditioned poem that was inspired by a *Cheers* episode.

Misery's Christmas, from Russia with Dog

Svyatoslav the sleigh dog lies dormant

beneath the holly hung at the children's orphanage door.

The gray-coated carolers of Minsk gather 'round the corpse,

hum in near silence for the dog-pawed, departed.

A seasonal mist congests both string and pipe-flute,

occludes the usual celebratory sonata.

Narek, the seven-year-old estranged minor from Armenia,

sticks the dead beast's burgeoning gut

with a chimney poker, then rejoices with hemispheric spirit,

At least this year, Pinata!

FAME ON YOU

FIQ QUICK QUIZ # 3

(Answers in the back! Answers in the back!)

9. Pretend to _____.

A. think nightmare you're living isn't real

B. miss pedestrians whose lives would make better headstones

C. care

10. Don't love people back; _____.

A. Pay that love forward. (Yuck, I could barely write it without hurling.)

B. Shave people's backs.

C. Get people back! (Choose this one, or go read Joel Osteen.)

11. Amount to _____.

A. a fifth of vodka

B. two-fifths of vodka

C. a hill of beans

12. Kennel your_____.

A. oats

B. neighborhood gays, I mean, strays

C. salivating fans, fool

RULE OF FAME # 13: LOSE YOUR PLUTO

By the 21st century, nobody, I mean no one was speaking of the solar system anymore, and that saddened me. Even the word *astronomer* had become so antiquated like word *apothecary* that you only came across it when reading Shakespeare at some used garage sale your aging mother forced you to go to while visiting over Mother's Day weekend.

Then, it happened. The planets lost their Pluto. When I first caught word of this, I thought Mickey Mouse and Disney Studio had lost their Pluto. But, like I told my folks when I fell in love with the puppy next door born on Christmas Eve, 1971. *The dog stays.*

Nope. The solar system had lost its distant, black sheep of a satellite. And when I read the scientific explanation in *National Geographic,* I never felt so stupid in my life. When perusing the edict released by the International Astronomical Union, I comprehended the words *with* and *the.*

Yet, Pluto strangely kept its inexplicable tie to Disney. It had become dwarfed. And I wondered. Does Snow White know? I mean, if there is no longer room in our solar system for 9 planets, how can we possible expect some infected-apple-ingesting princess of the woods to accommodate 8 dwarves? And what, pray tell, would the other 7 diminutive dudes name it? Jilty? Snubby?

At any rate, jilting Pluto brought the solar system back. Outer space had been missing in a black-media hole since *Star Wars, Close Encounters,* and *E.T.* It was the biggest thing of 2006 aside from Justin Timberlake getting *SexyBack.* Our universe had finally gotten its act together and sacked one of its own. And so can you....

Choose something that "sounds" near to you, but is really rather distant. In other words, you can live without it. Cut it out of the picture like an ex-lover in a good photograph, otherwise worth salvaging. Then, call the local newspaper with a bemoaning tone over the phone about your loss. That's it. Lose something trivial like a detestable sibling. Make a big deal about it. Then, publicize your grief. In a matter of minutes, you'll be surrounded by more suckers than are inside a piñata at Pepe's 8th birthday party.

RULE OF FAME # 14: START A BAND NAMED AFTER SOMETHING CONCRETE

The Doors. The Rolling Stones. The Velvet Undergound. Guns N Roses. Radiohead. The Supremes (if you count pizza)....the list of bands named after something concrete goes on and on. Forget abstraction when getting your gig together. When forming a hit music group, you have got to hit the public over its collective throbbing head with something concrete. Most people who are into rock music have rocks for brains. They respond to the hard and heavy. Get physical with feeble-minded fans and they will buy your band's albums like a gallon of gas. I myself am starting a band with a name that will harden in the noggin like wet cement in the Mojave. I am naming my band: The Bodily Fluids. I will be the lead singer and go by the pseudonym Spit Pittman. Our first album release will be entitled *Soul Secretions* and our first hit single, *Blood, Sweat, and Tears.* Sure, the song title is a rip-off from a late 60s band, but if anyone of the original band is still alive, who's going to bother to turn up their hearing aids, after years of speaker-blast concerts, to tell them while they're in retirement in some rock-n-roll retreat trailer park in the Florida Everglades? Copyright infringement is overrated. I mean…Did Pizza Hut ask Diana Ross & the Supremes if they could name their bestselling pizza after the most successful girl group in pop history? Nope. They just started hoisting cheap red roof after cheap red roof, spread out a lunch buffet, and were on their way to pan pizza fame. If the Nine-Inch Nails can do it, so can you. Think of something else hard that is nine inches and name your trio or quartet after that. You have to admit, it's pasta for thought that is bound to enlargen.

RULE OF FAME # 15: DON'T GIVE YOUR RUBES TO THAT BITCH WITH THE BROOM

You can learn a lot from Dorothy and her Oz-some adventures over that bow of rain. (1) Don't high-wire atop the fence of a pigsty just so three horny farmhands can cop-a-Kansan feel. (2) Don't run away from Auntie Em or anyone without checking the Weather Channel first, especially in the twister-challenged states. (3) Most importantly, don't give your shoes to that bitch with the broom. Houses fall in price in adverse markets, and houses fall on witches during bad-hair weather. Is that your fault? No. So if you've got any bling whatsoever on your body, don't give it to any bank, bully, boss, or bitch. You've got to cling to your resources like a sock caught in a static cycle. We live in a nation of takers, a world of wanters. And just as there is an **E-ON**, there is also an **F-OFF**. Getting robbed of your rubies before you've hit Fame Street is like conceding to a vasectomy just before you meet the Kate Middleton of your dreams. There goes your chance of producing a prince! Not to digress, but Kate Middleton is hot, Hot, HOT! Everytime I see her on the tele, I am reminded of that song, "Hot Cross Buns" and my London bridges start to fall down. I have a royal fantasy of my own involving a European tunnel as well…but to detail it would be to welcome bad taste.

Back to the subject at hand…If someone wants you to cough it up, remember…that's what phlegm is for…not what friends are for…. Possession is 9/10ths of the law…and the other $1/10^{th}$ is what lawyers are for. If you've got a full house—whether on the poker table, reality hit show, or black funnel over Emerald City—hold, Hold, HOLD…until you're darn well ready to drop on the witch, I mean wish, of your choice.

There's no place like home? Hmmph! There is no place like FAME! Home has mortgages and fires. Fame has prints of your feet and hands cemented in front of some Chinese restaurant in Hollywood.

And remember. The stairway to fame is not necessarily the stairway to heaven. You've got to watch every little step of your precious ascension, or you'll tumble out of the sky like a metallica zeppelin, a weighted down wizard balloon.

Your talent is your treasure. Protecting your emeralds isn't just for jockstraps and Spandex anymore.

RULE OF FAME # 16: DISASSOCIATE WITH LOSERS

That's right. You have got to get the "L" out. And I don't mean "lead out" or "Hell out." You have got to get the loser in you and the losers around you out of your pathetic life once and for all. Do you see the word "path" in "pathetic"? It is there as a root to let us know that the road to ruin is just one bad path away.

I've been surrounded by so many losers circling around me that I feel like a contestant on *Wheel of Misfortune*. The slow, the stupid, the complacent, the timid—all ringing around me like Woody's Roundup of Worthless People. I first noticed this in the summer of '69. And I am not talking about the c-o-o-o-l summer of '69 like in the Bryan Adams song and video circa 1983. I am reluctantly remembering the summer of '69 when my mother and I enrolled in my first summer of swimming lessons in a course called Mom and Tot.

Now, I was born blessed with athletic bones in every limb of my body. Obviously, I did not gather these genes from Mommie Dearest, or should I say, Mommie Drownust. Taking inaugural swimming lessons with her was like learning to paddle kick with the Liberty Bell. And, oh, there was a crack in it, alright.

I knew even before we got into the water that we were doomed for the depths of the Lamoni Municipal Pool. We lived near the pool at 115 West 10th Street, so we walked. (She walked better than she swam.) I was five and came head high to her waist.

We dressed in our suits at home. She "sported" a one piece that was dark chocolate with open-hole swirls across her midriff. If you have any mental imagery skills at all, you've already arrived at the fact the she looked like a Hostess cupcake.

Too bad she could not swim as well as one. The only thing she could do in a pool was sink. I swear, the woman swallowed more water than the hull of *Titanic*. She was so bad at body-boating that during a 15-minute reprieve, I slipped out to the office and asked if I could enroll in the just *And Tot* program. I mean, after all, I was swimming and shoveling along in the water like a dolphin on parade. After being told no, I resigned to the reality that I was stuck with this cream-filled sinkhole. And, sure enough, after six weeks, when the class results were posted, we had failed—the only Mom and tot slated to retake the course in the summer of 1970. It was then and there that I knew, although the lady could make a killer grilled cheese and tomato soup, she was a killer wail in the water.

Come summer of 1970, I dumped her like a truck dumps beach sand.

FIQ QUICK QUIZ # 4

(Answers in the back! Answers in the back!)

13. **Lose your _____ .**

    A. **Green card**

    B. **Temper**

    C. **Pluto**

14. **Start a band that's named after_____ .**

    A. **Any given deadbeat parent of choice**

    B. **Cement**

    C. **Something concrete (There's a distinction between B. and C.; and if you can't figure it out, you're too stupid to be famous.)**

15. **Don't give your shoes_____ .**

    A. **To the homeless unless with a tax-deductible receipt**

    B. **To joggers who trot by your home empty-handed**

    C. **To that bitch with the broom**

16. **Disassociate with**

    A. **all associations or anything that begins with *ass-***

    B. **those who suffer from dissociative disorders—let 'em wander**

    C. **losers**

RULE OF FAME # 17: IF THE KARDASHIANS KAN, YOU KAN

Life is replete with great mysteries: the creation of Stonehenge circa 2400 BC; the introduction of New Coke in 1985; and the acquisition of wealth and fame among the Kardashian family ever since this clan of witless wonders clobbered any vestige of dignity cable television ever had in 2007 with the show *Keeping Up with the Kardashians.*

Now, the secret to success for this family allergic to talent appears to lie within the letter *K.* I mean, K's are all over this family like a fat Kid on a caKe. It's all begins with key-kinfolk matron, Kris Kardashian. She must have picked up on the alliterative genius of her name and then passed it down to her ill-skilled daughters Kourtney, Kim, Khloe, Kendall, and Kylie. This family was lining up more KKKKKK's than a white supremacy rally. I admit the sound is catchy. I mean, if it worked for Krispe Kreme and Captain Crunch, why shouldn't this vacuous ménage of media menaces benefit from it and make a KKKKKKKilling.

KKKKKKK-ching!

I swear, I have grown bald scratching my head in bewilderment while trying to figure out just what the Kardashians have to offer mainstream society besides tele-veneral disease? They can't sing, can't dance, can't act, and argue like a bunch of cliché' spoiled rat packers. Now, some of the females have some nice kabobs, but I saw better on

Baywatch; and, after season 7, I saw better on syndicated reruns of the *Golden Girls.* And ex-daddy-O Bruce Jenner's face is so plastic, you could rearrange it and have a decent set of cheap patio furniture.

And still, America continues to watch this debacle of a dynasty like a kar akkident.

And why should we keep up with this lineage line-up of losers? Personally, I'd rather keep up with curvature of the spine, an endless stream of telemarketers, or Usain Bolt. Speaking of bolting, that is exactly what Kardashians do best! Have you looked at the family tree of this dross of descendants? Divorce seems to be the KKKKKKey to suKKess. More limbs on their genealogy branches have more XXX's on them than a pornographic film. Mom was married to the guy who got off O. J. You can't swing a dead cat without hitting an NBA player who went to the altar with one of her KKKKKids.

But, I've got to admit. The name is the Kool Thing— *Kardashian*—I think it means *one whose sprints in a race vehicle*—all the way to the banKKKKKK.

RULE OF FAME # 18: SERVE AS A JUROR IN A HIGH-PROFILE COURT CASE

If you think the key to fame is sitting across Anderson Cooper or Kathie Lee Gifford in a spotlight interview, then jury sitting in a case of parallel renown as, say, Casey Anthony or George Zimmerman is for you. Get in that jury's box no matter what the cost! Stuff the juror selection draw box if you have to. Any idiot can agonize over an eventual NOT GUILTY verdict while corpses disintegrate in their coffins, so why not you? Jurors in high-profile court cases have it made-in-the-anonymous-shadowy-shade.

All you have to do is (1) outrage the American public with a ludicrous interpretation of justice with absolutely no logical regard to the deceased or their families; (2) keep your shamed name anonymous with an intriguing code for yourself like Boob Juror # 36DD; (3) immediately make yourself available for morning-show interviews like the media whore you were born to be; (4) look good in dark back lighting and fogged-out face; (5) establish a conflicted, agonizing, pseudo-sympathetic tone in your voice; (6) keep the public outcry flowing by making such statements on air like "Oh, yeah, I'd let her babysit my kids. She's grown and gained from the loss of her daughter and biological extension." or "Sure, I'd give him another gun to watch over my neighborhood. No one on the planet would be more careful with a weapon now that Skittles and human brains have been scattered on the sidewalk." And, finally, forget conscience and common sense as you sit there in the courtroom with crossed legs while secretly googling publishers to contact you once you're out of the jury box and into fame's hot seat.

Babies and black boys may be down, but you're on the rise, sweet cheeks! I mean, why should you care if the killers you just let go are casually walking around an IKEA furniture store with a Starbuck's blend in their hands while furnishing their federally protected apartments with imported wicker. Yes, there may not have been enough evidence to convict, but it is evident that in this saccharine society, an artificial substitute for justice like you can be famous until the next mindless killing and subsequent thoughtless jury acquittal rears its venomous head from the cobra pot of American culture. Striking.

RULE OF FAME # 19: MESS WITH THE MESMERIZED

*Have you noticed how the font size and arrangement of this book
changes without any sense or consideration to the reader?
That's because I am messing with the mesmerized.
You are still reading this crap, even though I have insulted
everything and everyone you've ever cherished
and don't even have the decency to do it
in routine, readable font.*

*This is what I call…
messing with the mesmerized.
You see the word **mess** almost in the word mesmerized?*

*That is not by accident.
It is by fact-cident.*

*People don't need hypnosis.
Human breathing patterns alone are hypnotic.
You just need them to hypnotize your way.*

*Once they do,
mess with them like a food fight in an Army cantina.*

*Live your life like a traffic accident, and trust me,
folks will turn their heads…mesmerized.*

*Rock bands do it all the time.
They light a few sparklers behind them…
and sing* Dream On *or* Love Hurts…

*They next thing you know
fans are tossing their underwear and paychecks at them.*

RULE OF FAME # 20: SERVE BILLIONS

Being famous is like working at McDonald's. You've to be able to serve billions. Just ask my ex-girlfriend from college and the backseats that accommodated her during her estrogen frenzy of the mid-to-late 1980s. My God, the shrieks for more alone could've torn down the Berlin Wall! Who needed Gorbachev, Reagan, or Perestroika? In fact, the would-be famous could learn a lot from the standard hamburger at Mickey D's: Be cheap. Be accessible. And the public will unwrap you for a mere buck at any given moment. Exposure with condiments, baby. Now, that's a Happy Meal we all can enjoy.

McDonald's has everything to be famous and stay famous: clowns, arches, and free refills. So what are you waiting for? Put some goop on that mug of yours, arch your back, and be refillable. And, as Lady Gaga says, play the FameGame.

As you walk by, inspire the desire in people to want fries with you.

You, too, deserve a break today. Let that break be fame.

Just as bacon is no longer just for breakfast anymore,

fame is no longer just for fast food.

FIQ QUICK QUIZ # 5

(Answers in the back! Answers in the back!)

17. If the Kardashians Kan,

   A. Kansas Kan

   B. Armageddon with Komplete ApoKaplypse has begun

   C. You Kan

18. Serve_____

   A. Subpoenas to friends you know and everyone you meet

   B. A higher power in a lower district

   C. As a juror in a high-profile court case

19. Mess with_____

   A. The Messiah

   B. The Messenger

   C. The Mesmerized

20. Being famous is like_____

   A. Eating at McDonald's

   B. Holding up McDonald's

   C. Working at McDonald's

RULE OF FAME INSERT: STAND IN FRONT OF A WHORE-HAREM OF TWENTY-FIVE TO THIRTY DESPERATELY AGING, FORMER BEAUTY DIVAS HOLDING A SINGLE ROSE.

It is time for brute honesty, losers. I no longer believe in Santa Claus or timely rebates from those cute little tags on vodka bottles. I do, however, believe in Prince Farming. He lives in my home state of Iowa, and he is currently, deservedly the most famous face on network television and beyond: Chris Soules is his name, and you can't swing a slaughtered swine without seeing his shirtless, sweaty self on every Twitter account, Instagram, Facebook link, or Pinterest post.

Yes, Chris Soules from Arlington, Iowa, is *The Bachelor*! And he's taken to fame like a Berkshire takes to its own bacon. His premise is simple: he's a farmer in search of a wife. Hey, so is every overall strap hoisting up a bar stool down at the Lucky Dive, but Chris has got a gig... and it all began with pigs!

Now, I don't think Hollywood's new version of Babe is actually into pigs, unless you count those five hoofers who were last to the mansion in the final limousine. Did you see that fiasco on the opening episode? That poor driver, those poorer tires, trudging up the lawn, flattening their tired treads with each rotation while trying to deliver five more slabs on a hook...I mean dignified women of the 21st century from which Chris is to choose for eternal love and vittles fixin' back on the back forty.

But you've got to admit. These ladies have spunk. They also have no shame...but the sisters have spunk. Why, I haven't seen such back biting since my buddy Michael Vick and I were tossing greenbacks on pit bulls back in the day.

But I love Chris. I love him! Did you hear those pick-me-choose-me pork chops during the first installment of a most recent series? Those who were about to be chucked out of the trough were not in love with our Mr. Soules. In fact, none of those nameless faces were. My God! The producers didn't even give those manufactured half-actresses name tags so we in the audience could follow along! No, they might have been in love with the thought of being chosen in front of millions of viewers to stick around another round, or maybe they hated the thought of getting the hog-heave-ho so suey soon. My point is this: Can you name any them? No. But you know the bachelor, the dude with the rose.

RULE OF FAME # 21: BLUR THOSE LINES

If you're not thrusting to the beat of Robin Thicke these days, you're hips must be in traction. Just what DOES rhyme with *hug me?* Being vague is being vogue. The early bird may catch the worm, but the dumb bunny gets to swallow. Look what being androgynously challenged has done for the caqueers of Boy George, Annie Lennox, and former Vice President Dan Quayle? That's right. I've coined another new word... caqueer...*it means the livelihood of the professionally strange and ambiguous*. You can only leave people dead in their tracks if they don't know if you're coming or going...or in Quayle's case...what you're doing.

People I wouldn't touch with a ten-foot pole talk about my private life all of the time. The world is full of Curious Georges, and don't forget... Curious George was a monkey who sold millions of books. You know what drives people bananas? Not knowing what triggers your banana....That's what drives them bananas!

Look, if Robin Thicke, TI, and Pharrell can make millions selling digital tunes while crooning to topless models that they are good girls, the sky is the explicit-limit for anyone who can blur those lines. (Not to mention the song was allegedly snatched from a Marvin Gaye classic. SEE "Steal Everything" in PROLOGUE.) I recently read that Thicke called the mega-hit a *feminist movement* on a media post of the respectable *Huffington Post*. Ha! Former First Lady Hillary Clinton slapping the Commander-in-Chief for leaving a sling of below-the-belt spit on Lewinsky's dress...now that's a feminist movement! Bill should've kept those lines blurred. What a pea brain! They don't call it Little Rock, Arkansas, for nothing.

By the way, I was born on Hillary Rodham's sweet 16...put on the party hat, doll face, and let's party...I will show you my birthday suit if you show me the cougar in you. Everybody get up!

RULE OF FAME #22: IF YOU TWIT, OPEN A WINDOW

Fame is nothing to LOL about. SRIUSLY. Face it. Facebook is here today. It is like a social bank, and you need an account, a hefty one. And Twitter appears to be more than a temporary buzz. Now, I am no techno-bug, but we live in the digital age. And what better way to falsify yourself than through electronic print and visuals? Post an awesome pic of you back in the day. Lie. Lie. Lie. Because those Internet addicts out there will believe, believe, believe.

Facebook and Twitter are so popular these days they are both a noun and a subject. Friend and like until you are blue in the face. Put down that cappuccino at Starbuck's right now! Not another sip until you have Twittered and Facebooked worldwide about the teaspoon of Splenda you just added to your Caramel Machiatto. Nothing passes those lips of yours until it has gone viral first!

Now, repeat after me. I've just added a friend. And that friend is fame.

FAME ON YOU TWITTER PAGE

FAME ON YOU FACEBOOK PAGE

<u>RULE OF FAME # 23:</u>

STRIKE THE POT OF GOLD IN NE<u>POT</u>ISM!

If you can't make it on your own, make it off the good name, talents, and deeds of a family member. Look at all the nobody no-talents who have done just that. *Nepotism* is a five-dollar word that means "blood-is-thicker-than-water" favoritism. It is as pervasive as air or Angry Birds. Look at Miley Cyrus, for instance. She owes it all to Daddy and *Achy Breaky Heart*. If there is a poster princess for nepotism in this great country of ours, it is that noddin-her-noggin-like-yeah no-talent. Miley is short for mileage, and no one has gotten more mileage from a father's fame than she.

Ah, yes, the riches in relatives.

This hypocrite with a hair-don't releases the hit song *The Climb* while at the top of the pop world and tell us listeners struggling to keep our eardrums from breaking that it's The Climb? Miley Cyrus has had it handed to her with a celebrity silver spoon.

The only thing she'll ever climb is a stripper pole.

And don't get me started on *Party in the USA!* What a sack of shameless promotion. There she is in the back of a truck wearing short shorts that cover the upper –rib region—looking like a bale of hay in boots— Speaking of bails, the public should bail on her.

And just how does Miley wryly stay atop the pop music world? By sitting atop a wrecking ball wearing the birthday suit her father gave her—just like her career.

Cyruses are known for their tempers. And because I do not want Billy Ray to come out here and bust my Achy Breaky Bones, I better close this chapter and quick.

RULE OF FAME # 24: RENAME YOURSELF AFTER A CANDY BAR

If it's good enough for Eminem, it's good enough for me.
Snickers, that's what I would choose, as a stage name.
It's my favorite candy bar. Instead of applauding, fans would snicker
as I walked on stage. Come to think of it, most of them would anyway—

if I renamed
myself "Snickers" or not.

And if this world can make a Honey Boo Boo famous,

what's wrong with a Bit o Honey Boo Boo?

Or a Baby Ruth?

Finally,

Dolly Parton,

if your career ever begins

to disappear in the vapor

of the Smoky Mountains,

I suggest a name change:

MOUNDS.

FIQ QUICK QUIZ # 6

(Answers in the back! Answers in the back!)

21. **Blur those _____.**

    A. **Cocktails**

    B. **Breathalizer tests**

    C. **Lines**

22. **If you twit,_____.**

    A. **blame it on the person sitting next to you**

    B. **be the first one to say "Who let one"**

    C. **open a window (of opportunity)**

23. **Strike the *pot* of gold in....**

    A. **legalized pot**

    B. **potted plants**

    C. **nepotism**

24. **Rename yourself after....**

    A. **a sex offender**

    B. **chemical waste**

    C. **a candy bar**

RULE OF FAME # 25: BE A SELF-SABOTEUR

Life is a parade. Torch your own float. No one can go up in flames like a self-sacrificing flamer. That's right. Endanger yourself. Throw yourself up against identical financial institutions and call 911 if you have to. We all know people like this. And certainly you see the word *fame* in *flames* and *flamer.* The real tragedy to their demise is that most of tragic souls with a hint of masochistic jasmine behind each ear just haven't been able to bank on it. For my money, Casey Anthony is the epitome, if not poster momma, of the quintessential Self-Saboteur. She twisted her stories so much, every time you saw her on the tube, you just wanted to tell her, *Left foot green. Right hand yellow.* Oprah exposed her childhood wounds, and harpooned herself into a multi-billionaire media whale.

And she's been spouting at the blowhole ever since.

If I am being redundant, I cannot repeat myself enough. Lohan does it. Mel Gibson does it. Sounds to me like Elvis and Michael Jackson did it big time. Great skates, even Olympian figure skater Tonya Harding did it to fellow blader Nancy Kerrigan. Shed some blood into your own popularity pool, and the fame fin will come swimming up to you like the first day of feeding season off Florida Key West.

You know who is there for the fin-ale, don't you? Those who survived the preliminary fins, including their own. What I am saying is this: Bite your own damn thigh first before the bloodhounds slam at your gams. Just make sure the networks are watching with a first-aid kit and camera, kiddo!

RULE OF FAME # 26: MAKE YOURSELF A HERO SANDWICH

Want more bread with that fame? Make yourself a hero sandwich! Heroes are hard to find. They are not, however, hard to make up or put together like a six-inch sub. You just have to have the right ingredients, or, as I like to put it, the right **scene-gredients.** That's right. You've got to create a scene where you are a hero, one about whom people will talk for years. Oh, if life only had more runaway baby carriages and cliffs to it, this would be a snap. But unless you live near a pre-school dangling precariously off the side of the Rockies, the hero in you will need another plan. Instead of Plan B, think of it as **Plan Me.**

Unfortunately, being a famous hero is not necessarily easy, even in the manipulative sense. Look for people and atmospheres where there is dangerous, even reckless living—an endless stream of bananas peels on a floor waxed with Crisco and inattentive idiots willing to slip on them. That's when you make your move! People are in dire need of rescue. Just look at Bruce Jenner's facelift or anything on TVLand. You've got to tap into your inner Lassie and rescue any freak you see from making further fools of themselves. (And, yes, I know my pronoun doesn't agree with its antecedent.) But you will have to agree with me on this. It's been over a decade since 9/11 and this country is long overdo for another national tragedy (the U. S. hockey teams in Sochi notwithstanding).

Be prepared and take advantage. Grab your hard hat and axe, join the local fire department, hunker down, and pray for civil disaster.

RULE OF FAME # 27: BE NAMOUS

Make a name for yourself. Do something to become a household name like Pledge or LeBron James. Let's face it. Some birthright names are not worth the paper certificates upon which they were written. If this applies to you, change your name to something that rolls off the tongue like a meatball on a slide of spaghetti. It's bad enough being a loser, but having a loser name is beneath contempt. Georgios Panayiotou (George Michael) and Frances Gumm (Judy Garland) altered their namesakes, and the result was Wham! and Oz! Poor Judy. Her original name was a cross between a talking horse and connective tissue in your mouth. Now, changing your name usually involves a lengthy process including the proper forms, a notary public, and the clerk of court. It's sort of like divorce. You're divorcing the loser in you to become someone better, and that is something society desperately needs—less losers.

Being famous means being namous, just like being rich is being the niche. So move your moniker, change your nomenclature, trade your tag and bag fame like a grocery sweepstakes winner. If you don't have the dimes or the time for a full name change, at least invent a sobriquet that has staying power. And if you don't know what *sobriquet* means, you're not sophisticated enough for fame anyway.

What is good enough for Flo rida is good enough for me.
I am changing my name to Geor gia.
I will open At lanta, then take my show To ronto.
If that doesn't work, I'll change it again, something theatrical, like Usher.
No. That's already taken. I've got it. Projector.

RULE OF FAME # 28: DON'T GIVE A PENNY FOR YOUR DISTRAUGHTS

Few people care what you think, and even fewer care how you feel. This is a harsh reality, a bitter pill to swallow like bankruptcy or bloating. Do you see the word **press** in the word **depress**? Well, walk around like a sad sack on stage and that's exactly what you will be—without the press, or depressed.

Keep it light and meaningless like melba toast, the cast of *Jersey Shore*, any episode of *The Partridge Family*, or Nicole Richie's career and you will reach the heights of frenzied fame faster than Paris Hilton can scream *Orgasm* in any given video leaked by any given ex-boyfriend.

Leave the tragedies for the evening news, and you will find yourself featured on *Entertainment Tonight* a commercial break later—the subject of much trendier fare like celebrity inbreeding, adultery addiction, revolving-door child custody, and division of property in the greater Los Angeles area.

You'll hit the tabloids like Mike Tyson hit any woman he ever took out for drinks and dancing. You'll be on more magazine covers than Oprah's O-shaped lips forming the phrase **mOre mOney** on her own glossy of self-indulgence. And best of all, you'll have so many caboodles of cash that Bill and Melinda Gates will tap on your limousine window to bum a smoke or some spare change.

Cheer up, and as The Bard once put it, you'll be in the chinks!

FIQ QUICK QUIZ # 7

(Answers in the back! Answers in the back!)

25. **Be a Self-....**

A. cleaning oven

B. loather

C. saboteur

26. **Make yourself....**

A. invisible

B. out a check to cash

C. a hero sandwich

27. **Be....**

A. ware

B. have

C. Namous

28. **Don't give a penny...**

A. when a nickel will get you the whole night

B. when the nearest wishing well isn't within driving distance

C. for your distraughts

<u>RULE OF FAME # 29: YOU'LL NEED A THEME SONG</u>

Rocky Balboa had one, so did Barney, for that matter. If a theme song is good enough for a Philadelphia fighter who can't act or a purple mastodon who can't sing, it's good enough for you. (By the way, Beck's *Loser* has already been taken.) Fame requires consistency and motivation, and what is more consistent than a theme song or jingle about you that sticks in the minds of people's heads like Scotch on tape. Evita Peron became the most famous woman in the world besides Queen Elizabeth and those bosomed pin-up girls hanging on the walls of gas stations after World War II. Eva did this by addressing the entire country of Argentina and insisting they do not cry for her. Which, of course, they did. It was reverse psychology dished to the people below the balcony, you know, *beneath* her. Write your own words. Sing your own praises. Get to a recording studio and download to the masses writhing below.

Perhaps no other celebrity ingrained a theme song better than that twit Mr. Rogers, flitting in through the door and humming a few bars about the beautiful day in the neighborhood. It was ALWAYS a beautiful day in that neighborhood and he had the dry sneakers and sweater to prove it. Just once, I wanted that sap to come through that jolly door wetter than a T-shirt contestant babe on spring break at South Padre Island and say, *Damn, kids, that sure is a mother of a storm out there. We're staying the f**** inside and making Smores!

RULE OF FAME # 30: SEE YOU ON THE LATE SHOW

You can make a fortune off Americans' obsession with insomnia and staying up all night. Just look at what those monotonous logs, I mean, monologues, did for Carson, Leno, and Conan O'Barbarian. Not to mention Gee-I'm Failin, I mean Jimmy Fallon. Moreover, if you've got a product to pitch past midnight, call your local television station, fork over a few hundred bucks for the first taping, and start selling that snake oil beneath the midnight oil of lullaby lights, camera, and ultimate consumer dissatisfaction. I mean, if Cher can launch a comeback persuading women who are still awake at 2 AM to buy hairspray that isn't *schticky*, so can you! Letterman has left early; it is time you arrived late.

Case in point. My more cultured friends in Chicago have informed me of an Infomercial magnate, one Kevin Trudeau (not to be confused with either Pierre or Garry) who made a fortune off the sleepless from Seattle to Martha's Vineyard. Trudeau tried, and succeeded in selling everything: pain-relief adhesive tape (whatever that is), cancer-curing coral calcium (say that 3 times fast), and weight-loss books that endorsed prescription hormone injections, a month of egregious colon hydrotherapy, and a 500-calorie-per-day diet. Follow this guy's platform of pontification and you not only lose weight, you lose your shirt and life as well! I mean, this guy could sell outdated, imported Kool-Aid from the Jim Jones' Guyana Cult Camp circa 1979.

Thousands of cigars, furniture-filled mansions, and dapper designs for men later and Trudeau is on the run from the FTC with a $40 million fine trailing him around the world like a Sherlock Holmes' bloodhound. (Update: He's headed for jail time faster than you can say, *This product will work for you. I guarantee it!*) But it's elementary that he's famous... fraudulent...but famous, all because he posted some toothpicks between his upper and lower eyelids, drank caffeine until he himself was "Mountain Grown" and sold the snoozeless on a dream.

Fame is a lady of the evening

who works the bedroom before working those bank accounts.

So strap on that garter of earthly delights, bottle it, learn about PayPal and late-night programming...and, baby, you're an up-all-night star! Cash will come your way like breakfast in bed. They don't call it the Boob-Tube for nothing.

RULE OF FAME# 31: THE SIX PILLARS OF CHEATING

Character counts. So does a serial killer accruing dead bodies beneath the floorboards in a home that looks like Boo Radley used to ball-and-chain around. My point is this. Character is like any Big 10 football team in pre-season. It's overrated. And you cannot walk into any American public school these days and swing a dead mockingbird without hitting these six pillars of character: trustworthiness, respect, caring, fairness, responsibility, and citizenship. These, my fame friends, are your six tickets to Nerdsville.

Instead, adopt the six pillars of cheating. If it can work for Bill Belichick, Tom Brady, and the New England Hatriots, it can work for you. (1) It's not cheating if you don't get caught; (2) If caught, play dumb bunny. Be so dumb and bunny-like that Hugh Hefner will want to put a staple in your abdomen and make you a centerfold.; (3) Along those lines, defend yourself by claiming you didn't understand the rules. If that doesn't work, say the word *parameters*. People love words like *parameters*. It makes them think they're smart as they contemplate what the hell you just said. (4) Know as much as possible in advance. Cheat sheets just aren't for algebra and grammar exams anymore. Plans and answers are lying around everywhere. (5) Be prepared to eat the evidence. Good cheaters can digest shredded paper like shredded wheat. (6) Most importantly, flip it. Put the cheating blame on your accuser. Tell them that they cannot prove that you didn't win fair and square, BUT that you can prove they are a SORE LOSER. End your tirade by calling them a LYING SACK. Don't say anything after the word *sack*. Let their loser dirty minds fill the sack with imagery of choice, and we all know what word will go into that sack, don't we? Then, just walk away the lying, cheating winner you are, leaving the honest and sincere dead in their tracks holding a sack of *shhhh*—it will come to them.

RULE OF FAME # 32: IT WON'T MEAN A THING IF YOU AIN'T GOT THAT SLING

The world is filled with Armor Plates and Heavy Weapons. You couldn't ask for scarier barriers. In sum, let's call it humanity. From HOLLYWOOD to the Donald Trump Organization, there is so much red tape sticking and stabbing at your dreams that if you don't watch your ass, you'll look like a self-inflicted, mummified stop sign. Oh, sure, you'll stop traffic. But not in a good way. More like in the welfare way.

Writing this sensational, self-help memoir, I never thought for a moment that I would get Biblical on my readers, but, alas, my friends, I must dip to the Scriptures. Cut to *Samuel I* and the story of David and Goliath. Don't shut the cover! I know it's the most trite story in the Good Book. But what is trite can also be true….Now, Goliath was a force with which to be reckoned. (Notice how the preceding sentence absolutely refused to be ended with a preposition.) Oh, yes, Goliath…he stood 9-foot tall. So what! So did Alice tripping in Wonderland, and were any of us scared of that high-as-a-kite figment of Lewis Carroll's perverted imagination? I don't think so.

David wasn't intimidated by Goliath. That sheepish shepherd saw that Big Galook as keys to the kingdom, and, boy, did that future king open the door! David had equipment. Faith in God and a sling. And I'm not talking about the kind in which you place a pebble and fire away like a PEZ dispenser. That dude was packing, and he has the rest of the Old Testament to prove it. You have got to make that Go-liath into a Went-liath. History. Vapor.

King David is my idol. Well, he and a certain basketball coach from Ames/Chicago (whose name is too dignified to sully in these pages. Heartbroken Iowans will know why). They both are classy GIANT slayers who, as Teddy Roosevelt so shamelessly pilfered from the Native Americans put it, walk softly and carry a big stick!

Yes, the world is filled with judges, kings, false non-for-prophets, highly-recruited Kansas Jayhawks, and rabbits in hurry for a hole. Watch out, my tiny Alices! Equip with the abstract, Jack! Pack below the belt. It don't mean a thing if you ain't got that sling. And remember…

Fame is elusive as a rabbit. Go on and Grab it. Have a cotton ball!!

FIQ QUICK QUIZ # 8

(Answers in the back! Answers in the back!)

29. You'll need_____.

    A. a good agent

    B. a better attorney

    C. a theme song

30. See you _____.

    A. in prison

    B. at the front of the unemployment line

    C. on the late show

31. Cheating has six......

    A. siblings

    B. social diseases

    C. pillars

32. It won't mean a thing if you ain't go that......

    A. clearance clause

    B. severance check

    C. sling

RULE OF FAME # 33: ICONICIZE

The word *icon* has been through more changes than the weather, more changes than gowns worn by the host of the Oscars (pantsuits if we're talkin' Ellen), more changes than a chameleon caught in a kaleidoscope, more changes than a lightbulb in a Polack joke, more changes than Chastity Bono at a swap meet featuring androgynous articles of clothing formerly worn by lesbians who brought the whole lumberjack look back. Do you see where I am going here? Good. Because I don't. Oh, yes, the term *icon* historically meant a painting that venerated Jesus Christ or holy figure on wood traditionally used as an aid of devotion in the Byzantine or Eastern Orthodox churches. Cut to the 21st century, and *icon* is a pictogram stuck on some computer screen, so some illiterate can click on GOOGLE Chrome, or it's a former Disney Channel star (one whose fictitious first name was a barren Biblical figure and whose last name was a western state known for its after-hours activities with sheep) twerking at the MTV Video Music Awards while giving herself a Hannah-Montana with a foam finger. Oh, yes, Slimey Cyrus is so desperate to stay in the limelight that she shamelessly demonstrated her sexual coming-of-age with a football fan prop putting six in her end zone. And, boy, did Inchy, I mean, Miley, make the ESPN highlight reel for weeks for that artificial-index inspection.

If she ICON! You ICON!

Jazzercize. Supersize. Bette Davis Eyes. The "ize" have it. And for the 21st century, my friends, you must ICONICIZE. In other words, make a name for yourself that sticks to the public throng like Scotch Tape, like honey to your hair. By the way, do you know how to get honey out of your hair? With a honeycomb!

Use the name Veronica Velcro for starters. If that doesn't work, steal some cool name off Craig's List and spread it like fertilizer as if you were a lawn expert on a special segment of *This Old House.* That's it. Take your newfound nomenclature and toss in all four directions to the winds of fame. I mean, look what being named after a direction did for Kanye West? Or former *Dennis the Menace* star Jay North? Or *Games People Play* one-hit wonder singer/songwriter Joe South? And, last but not least, the Wicked Witch of the East?

Being an icon is making an indelible impression, a lasting imprint on the minds and mania of the masses. Envision yourself as a fully-treaded Goodyear radial tire making tracks down Success Street and leaving marks on the backs of your competitors. Madonna did! Ooops, different kind of marks on those backs (and I don't think they were wearing shirts....) Speaking of the Material Girl, I am borrowing from her as well. That's tight, I mean, that's right. I am releasing my debut album ***LIKE AN ICON*** with its title song subtitled (Worshipped for the Very First Time). I'll ask my buddy Kanye West if I can have that crown of thorns he wore on the cover of the *Rolling Stone* and use it as a chastity belt on my own cover, while I recline over an enlarged map of former Soviet satellite states among the throes of poverty and despair. Yes, ***LIKE AN ICON***. The release is going to spread like Chernobyl radiation. Russian President Vladimir Putrid will request a command performance of mine at Moscow Pie Palace. I will graciously decline for humanitarian reasons. I have a sense of them.

RULE OF FAME # 34: BE READY TO BE THROWN

Like the 1919 World Series or a rubber chicken at the state fair, the about-to-be-famous must be prepared to be thrown for a loop big enough to be the interstate exchange between the American and European continents. Fame is a mind scrambler, and you might as well be half-crazy and three-quarters cocked before you stake that claim to fame. Do you see the word **rat** in rationality? Rationality will gnaw at your chances of becoming infinitely famous like the sewer monger in the fissures of your half-baked brain that it is. Be ready to be thrown by throwing rationality and reasonable fear out the back window like the baby's used bathwater that it is, and you'll be fine. (I think.)

And you can forget the casket of wine, bucket of wings, and a blanket. Fame is no picnic. Speaking of wings, if I hear one more song about *Give Me Wings* or wind beneath someone's wings, I think I'll de-plane, parachute or no-parachute jump to that blissful state and place where songs about people's underflapping, flabby triceps cannot be metaphorically euphemized, or euthanized, as wings from heaven. If having flab behind each humerus bone were a ticket to God's blue sky, then every boothful of bloats at Hooter's stuffing their fat faces with buffalo wings and boobs...yep, those guys...are just a pitcher of Coor's away from meeting St. Peter.

But I digress. My point is...life is a track-and-field meet, you've got to be ready to be thrown like a discus through a dust bowl before you can golden-child anchor the 4 x 400 to Athenian glory and ultimate victory. That's right. Fame will toss you like a salad in a storm at sea. No one said pervasive popularity was smooth sailing. It's more like rough riding. So find the Teddy Roosevelt in you, cowboy, and get-a-trottin' toward a better horizon. And if your horse throws ya', good for you. Use it as experience for the throwdown showdown ahead at the O'Fame Corral.

Perhaps pop balladeer Michael Bolton said and sung it best in the Disney theme song from *Hercules*. You've got to go the distance, or at least be prepared to be thrown the distance. Before you can **hot-put** society, you've got to be the shot put of society.

Unlike my ex-girlfriend on any date from 1983-1985,

fame is **not** overnight.

It is over flight, and you're the UFO,

Unequivocally Fabulous Object of its desire.

We can't all be Kardashians. Bartender!

PART TWO: BE READY TO BE ENUMERATED AND EVALUATED

Test me. Rank me. Rate me. Weigh me. Be ready not only to be thrown, but also to be enumerated, evaluated, and outright judged by every a. h. with an opinion. If you can't abide the numbers' crunching, you might as well take a pass on being a passenger aboard the Fame Train. Or at least head back to the losers' caboose.

We humans have nothing better to do with our walk through life than to assign qualitative and quantitative measures and assessments on one another, or *data delirium* as I prefer to call it. This is considered normal. In fact, I think it's in the *Bible*—right next to the right to possess hidden assault weapons to brandish in front of some Brownie on your porch selling Girl Scout cookies. *I'll take two boxes, please!* Then, go for your gun as she goes to her pockets to make some change. Hey, you stood your ground and got some free thin mints and caramel de lite Samoas all in one pistol whipping!

My point is this...It is a thumbs-up and thumbs-down world. So, get your thumb out of asterisk *, take a number, and wait in fame's delicatessen line for your number to come up. Just make sure you've got some mighty fine meats and cheeses to offer when it's your turn at the display case, or the maddening, quick-tempered public will *throw* your scraps out the butcher's back alley for the hungry cats to devour—chew! chew!

Choo-Choo! This gets us back full circle, my fame trainees. Still on board with this! It's not too late to go home. Be ready to be tossed at any crossing! Just ask Shelley Hack, Tanya Roberts or any other *Charlie's Angels* replacement. Be prepared to be jettisoned when those rankings and ratings go down...down...down.

Be ready to be *thrown.*

RULE OF FAME # 35: CRASH, BURN, SHAVE, REPEAT

You know, Loretta Lynn and Britney Spears have a lot in common. One sings about ropin' goats, and the other croons about having sex with roped goats. And both divas from the country and hip-hop pop genres knew how to crash and burn in front of legions of fans, turning a rather susceptible moment into major bank and furtherment of their careers. That's right. I have coined a new word, or neologism, *furtherment*. It is the state or processing of furthering one's fame and fabulousness.

Now, Loretta did it at a concert. She had been on the road more times than a fleet of Indy 500 cars on their last lap and legs. Her trusty old band of ne'r-do-wells were striking up another Loretta lovely, when Miss Lynn herself struck out. Friends, this is the moment in *Coal Miner's Daughter* when actress Sissy Spacek goes for Oscar and gets it! She drops the microphone, cuts off the band, and then confesses to a crowd of faceless farm farts drunk on Miller High Life like these geezers were her most sacred page in her Dear Diary. She bluegrass-blabbers on about when she's not on the road making music, she is on some mattress making babies. Productive. At this point, all becomes a blur as she sways back and forth like a Supreme jealously adding the background vocals to Miss Diana Ross in *Baby Love*. Then, *S P L A T !!* Her face falls to the stage and that tasteless Grand Ole Opry gown is all taffeta and tears around her. It's a celebrity shot that photographer to the famous Annie Leibovitz forgot to take: *Country Diva and Beaver Tits-Up in Blue Taffeta at the Opry.* She missed the Pulitzer in Photojournalism there, people.

As excruciating, exhausting, and embarrassing as the entire ordeal must have been, at least Loretta had the sense to go all gibberish before she fades to gray in front of thousands of paid customers. It became more of a documentary than a *Is-there-a-doctor-in-the house* moment for her. For the first time in my life, watching Spacek re-enact the Nashville crash before Hollywood lights, I felt empathy. Thank God the moment passed, but I swear it was there.

Britney Spears became all the buzz years later (circa 2007) when she shaved her head to purify the puke that had become her personal life and recording career. When you can't cut good songs, cut gold locks and make sure the camera is there to capture or Hairless Krishna moment. The next thing you know, you've shed those Starbucks lattes, slowed down with a baby on board, buffed your hot bod into a slinky, sleazy one piece, climbed out of one manhole in middle of the street on Armageddon night, and (knowing Britney) right back down into another. And the *Femme Fatale* is back.

Being hairless is not being brainless. Sometimes you've got to shave to find the cure...or at least a despicable looking mole above the left temple that appears even more egregious on a buzzed blonde. Just as Lynn landed on her Honky Tonk hiney, Britney had speared her career by shear-clip genius.

And just like Loretta had it all filmed in a major motion picture, Spears' story of shears-to-tears appears to be headed for Hollywood as well. I hear Lamb Chop is going to double for the actual shaving sequence.

And if there have to be more retakes than a studio album rehearsal of any Spears album, so be it. It is all about CRASH. BURN. SHAVE. REPEAT. Baby!

RULE OF FAME # 36: NOTHING MATTERS AND WHAT IF NOTHING DID?

Character counts. So do serial killers accruing locks of hair on pin-up bulletin boards in secluded basements. **Ok, so I rinsed, lathered, and repeated the same topic sentence from a previous passage to fame.** Funtheless. It has been said that character is what you do when you think no one else is looking. Wrong. Grand Theft Auto is what you do when you think no one else is looking. Be a character. But don't worry about having character.

John Cougar's album circa 1981 said it best. *Nothing Matters and What If....* Cougar asserted this before he added Mellencamp to his stage name and nearly pink-housed, ruined his career. That rock-n-roller was more **cougar** than when my drifting-in-her-50s older cousin started showing her teeth to some thirtysomething dentist in middle-of-nowhere. I swear. Was that, *I want you to floss me,* she said while under the gas? And who cares if she did? Nothing is the abstract matter, and that's the matter that matters most. Keep that in mind the first time you flop in your FameQuest, and you'll bounce back faster than a Slinky sportin' a condom.

I mean. Look at Red Riding Hood. What road was paved with better intentions than her trail of coming-of-age muffins to Grandmother house? And God knows what the woodsman did to her before Grandma Greywolf ate her. I think we all missed the lesson from Hood's cannibalistic deflowering. Don't open the goddamn door when a stranger, with fangs salivating from his shower cap to his crocheted slippers, summons you to come in while he/she is lying in Grandma's Feather Bed. It's a crossover country hit that John Denver forgot to write before he went leaving on a jet plane...nosedive wise...for life. I hope it hurt so good.

FIQ QUICK QUIZ # 9

(Answers in the back! Answers in the back!)

33. I_____

    A. canticize

    B. raqicize

    C. conicize

34. Be ready to be_____.

    A. sued

    B. shunned

    C. thrown

35. Crash, burn, shave....

    A. retire

    B. regress

    C. repeat

36. Nothing....

    A. is not impossible

    B. minus nothing equals a Billy Preston hit song from the 70s

    C. matters and what if nothing did

RULE OF FAME # 37: MAKE LIKE A PIMPLE AND BREAK OUT

I never in my illustrious writing career thought I would pen this, but pimples are the precursors to fame. That's right. Zits are zealous, anxious to spread on some skin like a viral YouTube post, like any given Kardashian woman after any marriage has been nullified for the hapless publicity stunt it was. Pimples are the seed-oil to fame. They are fast, furious, and frenzied. They are the Paul Walker Mitsibishi Emo VII sprint-car(r)ing across your face. And just ask any pizza/crater face you've ever sat next to in morning algebra class, they gang up for a drive-by squirting and stay for the remainder of your adolescence, which is more than we can say for Tiffany, Martika, or Billy Gilman. Who?

My point is this: There's gold in them thar' social-network oil pores that are freely exposed to the public. Find your acne access of choice and break out.

RULE OF FAME # 38: DUCK YOU

The Robertson Family Dynasty on A & E, the University of Oregon Football Team, and—in a classical sense—Donald and Daffy. Apparently, you cannot become famous these days unless you duck yourself. I, for one, thought I had too much dignity and restraint to duck myself. Time after time, I opted to duck off! But as I was flipping through the channels one evening like a mallard of malaise and stale suffering, I received it— my duck calling. Watching that high-powered Duck offense out in the Northwest engineered by Duck signal caller, Marcus Mariota, followed by a high-power ratings show of *Duck Dynasty* out in the Louisiana Bayou, in which Si was ranting about stolen tires so hot the lug nuts were still blistering to his crusty touch—yes, watching these Dukes of Duck Hazards convinced me that I, too, needed to get ducked. But first I'll need a rubber.

A rubber duckie.

RULE OF FAME # 39 (AND HOLDING LIKE JACK BENNY) :

LIVE LIKE YOU WERE DYING (YOUR HAIR)/JUST FOR MEN

I am allergic to adulthood. It is clearly for grown-ups, and I just cannot cut it. To make matter worse, I am currently battling the bottle: the bottle of men's hair-color products. (Let's just leave it at that.)

If patience were cash, I would be strapped like a death-row prisoner to a charged chair. Speaking of death row, impatience almost took me there shortly after my 49th birthday—or at least death's couch. Fame and gray hair do not mix. Fortunately for me, hair-dye liquids do. I have been foam-bombing my head now for a couple of years. I used to use women's hair coloring products from Loreal because they worked better, and frankly, I'm worth it. Then Combe Incorporated released **Just for Men** hair color, or what I prefer to call **Beauty in a Box**. This stuff magically morphs from liquid to foam with a squeeze. I was in hair-color heaven. Good-bye to grays and good riddance. When I first applied the dye back in the day, I failed to lube around the perimeter of what's left of my hair line and stained my ears. I looked like a bat out of a bottle, if you know what I mean.

To make matters worse, the next time I applied the scalp paint, I couldn't open the danged aluminum foil package with my slick fingers, so I just impatiently gnawed and gnashed the silver bag with my teeth.

Can you imagine what happened next:

Accidental Poisoning, or, shall I say, Near Accidental Poisoning. The liquid dye cream burst open in my mouth. Quickly, I read the instructions. You know the cautionary ones you're supposed to read before you open something toxic. Well, that's exactly what I read. HIGHLY TOXIC. Call Animal Poison Control if swallowed. I walked into the living room, which I thought quickly would become the Dying Room, sat and the coach and waited to be called Home. I thought about calling a vet, but what would I say? A load of cream made from Just for Men just went off in my mouth? Humiliating. To make an embarrassing story end,

I survived. Rinse. Spit. Repeat. You know how it is. But as God as my witness, I will never hair-dye again, unless I want to him-die.

RULE OF FAME # 40: HELL IS FOR REAL

I cannot speak for that kid who has made millions of dollars for himself and his family by claiming the same thing the *Bible* has been trying to do for, say, around 2,000-plus years: *Heaven Is Real.*

But I can assure you one thing, readers—*Hell Is for Real.* Trust me. I've been there and back on several occasions. In fact, I've been on so many hikes to Hades I am in its Frequently Frier Club. I cannot tell you how many out-of-body-experiences I have had after being so burning mad at what has happened to me here on Earth that I have found myself licked by flames. **Note:** How closely similar *flame* and *fame* appear. That's right. You get the "L" out of *flame.* And you have found fame. And isn't that what it's all about!

I don't know if the rest of this great nation of ours has 4-H, but here in Iowa, we do. It's an agricultural organization for youngsters, which stands for *head, heart, hands, and health.* But I am just-barely living proof to tell you, 4-H stands for Hell, *Hell,* **Hell, _Hell!_** I am shamrock-shaking as I write this: the trauma, the secrets, the insurance checks, aka, hush money put into my kiddie account at our local bank. I can no longer remain silent. If I don't speak for those cows, who will? Looking back, what didn't hit the proverbial fan during my 4-H ordeal? At the risk of being subjected to litigation, let's just say a certain close relative and his cruel cronies (who collectively had the IQ of the average nightfall temperature of Anchorage, Alaska, in the dead of winter) tossed and locked me into a grain silo for hours upon endless hours. There I was, splayed out like a poncho trying to dry after a rain soak. I knew if I tried to stand up and "walk" across the corn and other cereal fragments that I would sink like an environmentally-challenged elephant in the only quicksand found in the jungle. And my poor club calves—bludgeoned like baby seals along the Arctic shore—a shore that was the boundary between me and those 4-H heathens. Needless to say, my folks withdrew me from 4-H like a libertarian eventually withdrew from me any given election... Well, they withdrew me fom boys' 4-H anyway. They put me in girls' 4-H, so I could remain eligible for the county basketball tournament, being the best baller for my age south of the state capital.

Ah, girl's 4-H...where I was known for my Hello Dollies, a brownie-like bar made out of chocolate chips, sweetened milk, and other rich stuff. It's like sausage. You really don't want to know how it is made. Pat Benatar once sang that *Hell is for Children*. I think we Iowans should make her an honorary, lifetime member of 4-H. That's right, fame fenders, Hell is for real; and, apparently, its origins are the American family farm.

My point is this: Just as Colton Burpo, that little kid back from the dead in *Heaven Is for Real*, has seen Jesus, so, too have I had face-to-face encounters with the Devil. Most of our stereotypical images of the Devil are, in fact, true. He is red. He has horns. He is mad most of the time. He looks a lot like my now defunct father, but with a pitchfork rather than a steak knife. Oh, and the Devil wears shorts, sandals, and shades. It's hot down there for him, too—except they pronounce *shades* as *shay-des*, to rhyme with Hades.

FIQ QUICK QUIZ # 10

(Answers in the back! Answers in the back!)

37. Make like a pimple and _____.

    A. make a dermatologist's career

    B. make about $125,000 a year

    C. make out, I mean, break out

38. Duck _____.

    A. incoming plane

    B. or die nasty

    C. you

39. Live like …..

    A. you were dying (to meet the Olsen twins)

    B. you were dying (to touch a hair lock of any living Beatle)

    C. you were dying (your hair)

40. Hell is for….

    A. play

    B. tea

    C. real

RULE OF FAME # 41: HOLD THE WORLD FOR RANSOM

Fame is a river; and if you're a fisherman worth your hook and line, you've got to lure and snatch. It all comes down to this: kidnap or be kidnapped. If you're not abducting the public, you're just not trying. And once you're famous, let your autograph be your ransom note. Life costs. People have to pay. So why not pay you? Buy my CD. Visit my website. Follow me down this digital dark hole. You know how to do it. Common people are strings to be wrapped around the fingers of the famous. The masses are but dirt on the floor to be swept away by your sensationalism. You've got to fool folks into thinking that they are the treasure, and then pirate the public away, and put them into your Chump Chest where they belong. Trust me. They will never know what hit them.

Ransom rhymes with handsome, just as beauty rhymes with duty. Do you see where I am headed here? Fame has no place for people who should be walking around with potato sacks on their heads. You need a face that Van Gogh would want to paint (not the face Van Gogh sees in the mirror) or Michelangelo desires to chisel.

Just as we are putting more and more artificial substances into our food and diet, you will probably need to plastic that disaster of an appearance of yours before anyone wants to place you in front of back lighting for a photo shoot. For people to obsess on you, you've got to fix the mess of you.

I, too, was a kidnap victim as a child. Church Camp, Stewartsville, Missouri, circa 1976. Some whack job in our cabin who thought he owed it all to Charles Manson held the rest of us boys at squirrel knife point during afternoon siesta time. He was nuts, pun intended. There we were in our skivvies, all the kids shivering in fear for their 12-year-old lives. Not me. As I may have mentioned before, I am afraid of everything which makes me afraid of nothing. I was livid. If this nuthatch didn't release us soon, we were going to miss Canteen. That was the summer Starbursts came out, and I was addicted to strawberry. I tried to whisper and motion for the others to grab a mattress from one of the top bunk beds, and we'd dive on and smother the dude like gravy on onions. But did those Fruit-of–the-Doomed adolescents listen to me? No! It wasn't until the camp minister cut his way through a screen door that we were free at last...but too late for a Canteen pass. Those stars had already burst inside some other kid's mouth! Captivating the world means capturing the world, so climb inside your fame van and collect chumps like Pokemon cards, Clyde.

RULE OF FAME # 42: STAY HUNGRY FOR THE GAMES

I cannot get my fill of the *The Hunger Games*! Thank the ambrosia gods that it came with seconds and thirds, *Catching Fire* and *Mockingjay*. I mean how many of us get to die for a breast pendant? Or to provide week-old rye bread to our ribbed-caged families by killing all adolescent on-comers? It is a middle-school librarian's blue-haired, gray-eyed dream. Like the booty on J-Lo, people are checking it out.

You've got to hand it to, or perhaps stomach it for, author Suzanne Collins. Not only does she wipe the butt of the world from Harry Toileter, I mean Potter, but she holds a mirror-mirror in front of our collective cultural faces that exposes us for the evil queens with the poisoned apples that we are! (1) We tolerate and promote a winner-take-all mentality, aka, it's Tournament Time! (2) We encourage, if not downright force, our youth to compete for our vicarious-veined old selves. And (3) we are so addicted to reality television and social networking that we don't realize what heartless, personality-less zombies we've become! OMG! LOL! Put me in the remake *Thriller* video!

My point is this. If indeed the apocalypse is coming and we find ourselves in shantytown districts wrestling with reservoir dogs for scraps of jump drives and used spoons from Ben and Jerry's, it is best to burn for the flames of fame! If it worked for a girl whose name sounds like genus/species nomenclature for a feline-food fir shrub, Katniss Everdeen, it can work for you! So step into your trilogy of choice, and fame-famer-famest away!

<u>RULE OF FAME # 43: PATIENCE IS A VULTURE</u>

You read the title right. Forget every maxim, axiom, or dictum you ever heard about patience being a virtue. Patience is a vulture—a vicious, voracious predatory bird swirling around your slow, simpering self and just waiting to drop like a chandelier on its last hinges. If you think that all you have to do for the fame front to finally blow your way is to be patient, then you might as well start looking for the lever to pull to be crushed by a safe falling from the cloud banks of the sky.

Now, that Oprah Winfrey was one clever, ravenous old bird. She didn't wear a table-waiting apron for long before she was on national television daily speaking and weeping openly about cousinly relations that were, shall we say, too close for comfort. Next thing you know, she's on her own magazine cover every month and jet-setting out the Academy Awards every year. By the way, I think the *Wall Street Journal* should emulate Oprah and put a picture of the actual Wall Street in New York on the entire upper fold of its newspaper, each and every day.

Do you almost see the word *patsy* in patience? Patience hovers like some craft vehicle in an unpublished George Orwell novel. Its evil, eagle eye sees everyone standing in line as a road kill candidate. Oprah didn't wait. Justin Bieber was barely out of diapers before he took to the stage and made an entire nation nauseated.

Yes, indeedy, patience is a vulture that views you as its turkey, basting in mediocrity and good measure. And it loyally flies in a ferocious family circle with its career-killing kin—hope and delay.

So get panicked, get pumped, and get off that dark, desert highway if you are able.

People who wait...wait tables.

RULE OF FAME # 44: TPFF

I am **TPFF**—too popular for Facebook, too sensational for social networking. There, I've said it. But that doesn't mean other socially-challenged souls can't post up there like a 7-foot center for the Kentucky Wildcats who's going to play his Freshman year, take them to the Final Four, choke in the national semi's, and still rake in millions when junior is the number one pick in the NBA draft, at the ripe old age of 18 months. Social networking is an outrageous violation for those of us who want to be alone. The Greta Garbo greats, like me. Stay away from personal profiles on Internet and World Wide Web. Notice the words **net** and **web** in these phrases? That's because they are traps in the Digital Forest. You are not a fish; you are not a spider. You are human being short on publicity and longing for fame. I don't even know what being SKYPED means, but it sounds like it involves hair loss; and I need all of the head hosiery I can muster.

And I swear, so help me, if one more SNAP (Social Network Addicted Person) comes up to me asks if I've seen the latest pictures of them on Facebook, I am going to post my fists all over their skinsaver. I mean, it's bad enough I have to look at you in person. Why would I want to waste perfectly good gigabytes to do the same?

Facebook needs a reality check, some truth-in-friending competition. I've got it! Mirrorbook. On second thought—too many computers would crack.

FIQ QUICK QUIZ # 11

FAME ON YOU

(Answers in the back! Answers in the back!)

41. Hold the world_____.

    A. responsible

    B. accountable

    C. for ransom

42. Stay hungry for _____.

    A. Tibet

    B. dessert

    C. the games

43. Patience is a ….

    A. pain in the –ence

    B. pat in the pants

    C. vulture

44. TPFF stands for….

    A. Thank Prince For Friday

    B. Treat People Forever Falsely

    C. Too Popular for Facebook

RULE OF FAME # 45: ROOT FOR THE SHARK

JAWS I

You can learn a lot about fame from a mindless man-eating machine. You need to become fearless. As noted, I am so phobic of everything, that I've become immune to fear and have begun cheering for those objects and objectionables who terrorize me most, namely Great White Sharks. Now that I am on the shark's side, I've seen true light, or the true Great White: Eat or be eaten. Most of those people out in the ocean of things shouldn't be dog-paddling around that big blue basin anyhow. If God had wanted us to be in the ocean, he wouldn't have invented the city pool or *Shark Week* on the Discovery Channel. I can think of no better way to spend the first week of August each year than locking my apartment door to the world for a week, grabbing a big bucket of popcorn, stacking the refrigerator full of Skinny Cows, and sitting in front of the tube and cheering on the sharks as their natural habitats are being invaded by pesky scientists and ridiculous thrill seekers. Next summer, I am stealing a megaphone and some pom-poms from my school and doing cheers with stunts to encourage those sharks to do what comes naturally—kill, kill, kill!

JAWS II

When I was little, my older brother treated me like garbage that keeps blowing back into the yard—or else he ignored me. He always used to sing this song *No Time Left for You* by the Guess Who to me. No time? I didn't even know he could tell time! Some of the lyrics, especially "on my way to better things" left a permanent bruise in my soul. Not that I wanted to spend more time with that mistake at birth, I just didn't want to be rejected or ignored. I'll never forget—summer of 1975. Everyone, but my workaholic father, went to Estes Park, Colorado, for vacation to see my favorite aunt, Bert. I was 11 at the time—a horrible and harmful age at best. Wheeling out of the driveway that morning in June, I thought to myself, *Great…this family doesn't hike, ski, or mountain climb. What in the world are we going to do for a week in a ski resort in the dead heat of summer?* To make matters worse, my older brother decided to bring his best friend, Eric, with him. Tragic. When my oldest sister wasn't making out with him in the back seat all the way through Nebraska while the rest of us pretended to look at the passing wheatfields, Eric and my older brother downright ignored me. When we finally arrived in Colorado, all I wanted to do was do what every other red-blooded American was doing that weekend: Stand in line for 8 ½ hours to see Steven Spielberg's **Jaws.** I had been in line at the Estes Theater for about an hour, when I felt a tap on my shoulder. It was my oaf of a brother. He and his boob-best friend forced me to go back to the Holiday Inn, which, to this day, I argue is a form a kidnapping, since they weren't my parents. I was grounded on the spot and told not leave my hotel room for the rest of the day. So I decided to disappear—under the bed. I must've fallen asleep under there because hours later, I woke to this sobbing. My mother was in a state of shocked oblivion crying out for me, *Where's John? Where's John!* At about that time, I wished I had been eaten by a shark. Suddenly, I winced at a flick of light as my brother flung the blanket off the bed and started pulling at my left sneaker. I grabbed a couple of bed support boards and clung to dear life. There was no way I was going to let that sack of *(*()*()@# drag me along hotel shag carpeting like a shot-and-bound carcass. Just then, I heard creaking and breaking. The bottom bed boards were coming apart at the nails and seams. I heard someone cry out, *The bed is falling on John.* There I was…crushed under my own devices. I'm told my mother wrote the Holiday Inn a $600 check for the bed…and we were so out of there.

JAWS III

Circa 1975, I was so terrorized by *Jaws* and family drama that I could not let my feet stick out over the bed or my bean bag chair without waking up screaming that my legs had just become a couple of beef jerky sticks for a Great White. You know, like that crazy Alex Kintner kid on the yellow raft in the actual flick. What an idiot, beating the surface of the water with his shins, practically summoning the big white lug to feast on him. That's it, Alex, let's make a pow-wow call for the biggest maneater known to man. And don't even get me started on his out-to-lunch mother, Mrs. Kintner. There she was on the beach, in her big yellow flop hat (which by the way color matched her son's raft until the finicky fin dowsed it with the kid's own red blood)—yes, there she was lying on the sand like a pruning log and reading a magazine or something while her son was being torn into a wave buffet before millions of shrieking film fans— including myself. To this day, every time I dip into an ocean, I just expect to be ripped to shreds. It's really no different than the feeling I have entering the classroom each morning.

RULE OF FAME # 46: YOU'RE GONNA NEED A LARGER LIFEBOAT

You can learn a lot about fame from the sea, especially when Hollywood sets its floating cameras on it. Take *Jaws* and *Titanic* for instance. What timeless messages were taught from the bitten and frostbitten. Sharks come with their own salt. People come with their own ketchup. Think about it. And lifeboats on a sinking ship are like a restaurant that won't take reservations: first come, first served. And to mix a metaphor here, folks, to avoid trademark litigation from either film camp: *You're Gonna Need a Larger Lifeboat* applies here. That quote is right up there with *Frankly My Damned, I Don't Give a Dear!* and *Play It Again, Piano Man* as cinematic lines to live by.

Back to the shark. Now, Sheriff Brody (played to perfection by Roy Scheider) was so scared and numbed, he could only say it once while staring dazedly toward the ocean's horizon, cigarette askew and hanging in his dropped jaw like a stocking filled with enough coal to light up an NBA Scoreboard.

Speaking of dropped jaws, you've got to drop jaws of those around you and the general public. And the most manifest way you can achieve this is through materialism, i.e., a bigger floatation device. Do you remember the candy bar floating in the pool of *Caddyshack*? Crap floats. Just make sure yours has a large lifeboat hinged to it when Moby's Dick begins to shift. I know I'm mixing metaphors, but you're just going to have to sift through this one.

Now, Madonna lied when sang about being a virgin, pinched for the very first time (for the very first time since shop class); but she was right as rain when she mused that we are dwelling in a materialistic world…and the boy with the most toys wins. Forget your feelings and the feelings of others and start mounting material things like your first name was *Rush* and your last name was more, More, **MORE!!!** Presidential sweet!

A bigger boat? Buddy, you're gonna need bigger fins for this swim. Begin by enlargening your resume'. ***Buy pills on-line if you have to***. Now, sit back and admire the word FAME swell and sell in ALL CAPS.

RULEOF FAME # 47: MAY THE SCHWARTZ/WARTS BE WITH YOU

Just as you will need a bigger boat, you are also going to need a smaller sidekick. You know, you're all-around inferior person who, merely by standing at your side, makes you look and feel better than you have a right to. Batman had Robin; Jordan had Pippen; Nixon had Ford; and I have some former student sap whose name I will protect out of respect. We'll call him Everett Schwartz. This guy follows me around like a shadow selling Super Glue.

He's always there for me like an overdue bill, a recurring rash.

His senior year, he signed up for my first-period class, which then had to be renamed Morning Sickness 101. I'd tell him to get lost, but he wouldn't know the way.

I am three times older than he is, and four times better—at everything. This consolation runner-up must have been exactly what Clint Eastwood's Dirty Harry was looking at when he glared and stared, *Go ahead, make my career*!

Ever Warts (my nickname for him) is forever-there to keep the popularity pots a-stirring at a rather hectic workplace that appears to have a rocket symbolically perched skyward in its front lawn. (I can't tell you how many times I've wanted to strap or straddle myself onto that booster launch and head for the moon on a bad Monday. But I digress.)

At ball games, it's Wartsy who gets the student section to chant my name, even the haters! It's like we're both a part of our own Great Lake System. He's Eerie and I'm Superior.

This reminds of the time my Dad was driving us kids around for another Sunday Cigarette Smoke Fest in his Brown LTD. He was mad at me for the millionth time that weekend and finally turned his fuming face precariously toward me…quivering in the backseat. And he said, *John Goddamnya, you're not happy unless everyone around you is equally unhappy as well.*

And I abruptly retorted to that trauma-head-missing-one-tractor, *Oh, really, I didn't observe any equals around me!*

Thanks for the miseries, T. Revs. I mean, memories. Now, go peel me a grape!

RULE OF FAME # 48: IN PRAISE OF BAD PUBLICITY

In the Sea of Celebrity, bad publicity is the Loch Ness Monster. It doesn't exist. People claim they see it, but just as its neck surfaces, it vanishes--and only the claim remains. And, folks, it's those claims that are famous. My point here is this: You don't need a big foot; you need a big story. Just as there is no such thing as a bad fur wrap, there is no such thing as a bad rap...period.

Blame it on the Bieber. After recording bad song, after bad song, he took his maladjustment into manhood and monotone voice to the streets where he continues to make headlines accruing traffic and indecency tickets like a pigeon gathers crumbs in your New York park of choice.

If you fall to pieces, do so in front of a photographer and reporter. (It spear-headed Britney's wallowing career.) A would-be famous person who falls in a forest is like solitary tree itself that takes a tumble. Who hears it? And who cares? When hikers, rangers, or worse, lumberjacks do find it, they just chop it to pieces and make the evening's kindling. Crack before the camera, or for God sakes keep it together!

RULE OF FAME # 49: BUILD A FAÇADE, AKA, A FAKE FRONT

Happiness comes from within, so does the intestinal flu. No one really wants to know the real you, so keep your sorry self to yourself and concoct someone fabulous—and fake. You will be glad you did.

The words *fake* and *fame* are kissing cousins, closely related. So are the words *interior* and *inferior.* So if you want people walking all over you like a doormat at Grand Central Station, open up to the them. But remember this, fools. People who open up need to prepare for one thing: **invasion.**

Instead, build a nice storefront, a fine dress window that people like to hover around and point and wish for the things they see. Every few weeks or months, change what is shown in the fake dress window that is your social personality. People will become intrigued wondering who or what they observe next.

You don't have to be you unless you choose to be you—and that's just wrong.

I tried being one of those sincere people, and all I received was emotional treadmarks from people racing all over me like I was the track at the Indy 500. I only became confident when I stopped confiding in people. There is no shame in being sham. Even I don't recognize myself anymore, and I couldn't be happier. I have built a wall around the true me that idiots keep bumping into and don't realize they've just been whacked by my social stack of bricks. This is a driving force in playing the fame game for me. By constantly changing my exterior, I am able to assess what the public wants to see and who I should be for just that moment.

Choose to be a rerun, and that is exactly what you will be: run-over.

RULE OF FAME # 50: ALWAYS LEAVE THEM WANTING MORE

Crowds are chumps. They are! Just ask Don Henley and the Eagles on any given night the group members were too crocked up to know the difference between Hotel California and Winslow, Arizona. Fans are your servants. Why do you think they call it *Ticket* Master? Any collective group of people willing to pay and sit in the dark for a few songs or chuckles is Silly Putty in your hands. What are you waiting for? Get molding! Plaster the grandstand gullible, then peel them back to expose them for the comic-strip kazoos they are...but first...take note of this. Like a surprise guest whose presence, at first, evokes grins and giggles, never, ever extend your stay on screen, field, or stage. Leave the watching... wanting more. They will. If check out is at eleven, exit at ten. End of story. Almost.

I have a built-in sonar/sound detection like a Meatloaf bat-out-of-Hell song from the 70s. And, trust me, once the crescendo of applause wanes like a tide receding to expose the bald shoreline, I pull out like a backseat Buck who forgot his Trojan before mounting the whore, I mean, horse. Fame is not about talent; it is about timing. I sense things. I do. Intuitive. People are social selves...so is horse crap left behind on Main Street during a Fourth of July parade in Pleasanton, Iowa. Trust me, that is one pitched stick of Laffy Taffy you do not want to pick up from the concrete. And if you can't sleep with the powers-that-be, CREEP with the powers-that-be. They're snakes, and they know it. Glide through the grazing grass with them...then slither out...leaving their serpent saliva wanting more...More...MORE!!! Remember. You're nothing if the general population does not demand a sequel. I mean, look what sequels did for *The Godfather* and Twinkies. Mick Jagger said it best, *Don't give them any satisfaction.* Then, sing and howl about it all the way to the top of the *Billboard* chart. And you will be riding atop the wave like that surfer girl in Hawaii who got a bite from a shark, then turned it into a bigger bite of fame. It's all about the finish, baby, and do you see the word *fin* in *finish?* Great white sharks can, and they're legally blind by ocean standards. Go in the water. Momentarily. Just leave the wet saps in there while you towel off in time for happy-hour martinis with the lads from Lincoln Park. Love you, Kent and Clay!

Study Adele. (And if she doesn't diet soon, there is A LOT there to study.) I love Adele. She pleases her crowd while crooning about rolling in the deep and loving someone like you, then disappears into the stage vapor, leaving the crowds at Royal Albert Hall or wherever chanting her name and demanding more of her essence. Meanwhile, she's back in the exit alley chain-smoking like the poster child for hand-to-mouth disease while an open-door limo waits to whisk her away to fame's frontier. She may be only 19, 21, or whatever post-adolescence number she entitles her next smash album, but Adele is the Channing Tatum of lounge lizards with a helluva voice. A big-time crowd pleaser who always leaves them fist-in-dollars wanting more. Just don't give her a stripper pole, a dance troupe, and Ginuwine's *Pony* song to gyrate those big as a *hills-are-alive-with-the-sound-of music* British hips of hers as a warm-up.

FIQ QUICK QUIZ # 12

(Answers in the back! Answers in the back!)

THE LAST QUIZ

(Oh, and this is the back. All of the answers were C.)

45. **Root for the** _____

    A. hair follicle   B. Alex Haley sequel C. shark

46. **You're gonna need a larger**_____

    A. moving van   B. complaints box   C. lifeboat

47. **You're gonna need a smaller**

    A. traceable bank account B. cemetery plot C. sidekick

48. **Praise**_____.

    A. Yeezzuss B. bald puppetry   C. bad publicity

49. **Build a** _____.

    A. better you B. open door with doormat C. façade (fake you)

50. **Always leave them** _____.

    A. in the lurch   B. begging for breath C. wanting more

THE END

(THAT'S WHAT THE PRODUCERS OF THE FIRST *FRIDAY THE 13th* SAID.)

RULE OF FAME # 51: DO MORE THAN EXPECTED

I know. I know. I just advised you to always leave them wanting more, and the cover material of this runaway bestseller reads that there are 50 ways to make you famous. All of this may seem antithetical, hypocritical even confusing to you.

I don't care.

You're still reading this stuff, which means you've got more to learn, and I have got more to show and tell.

People love extras. Extra cheese. Extra mayo. Extramarital affairs.

It's in our bloodstream to pump more, more, more out of a resource. And, my little Helen Kellers, you have come to the right well to apprentice the waters of fame. (Doesn't count as a Helen Keller joke, so just get over it.)

Imagine how much better it would have been to read under the bed sheets about *51 Shades of Grey,* sing about *52 Ways to Leave Your Lover,* or finally allow Puerto Rico or Mainland China to become the 51st state of America!

If you still feel betrayed by hypocrisy and doublespeak, just look at what both of those contradictions of communication did for the Bush and Clinton dynasties, not to mention Frank and Kathie Lee Gifford. We're talking Oval Offices and talk shows here, people!

Do you see the word *ore* in *more* and *encore*? Fame is a rock that you've got to mine, Mine, MINE, to extract the last valuable vestige of a mineral from those who are paying to pay attention to you. Do you see the word *extra* in *extract*? Do you see the word *mine* in *mineral*? Your fan base is a quarry; and, believe me, most are as dumb as a box of rocks. You are Led Zeppelin.

Ore is it Lead Zeppelin?

And I don't care if I am mixing metaphors here. Withhold and then unleash your *Stairway to Heaven* just when the crowd of blood clots thinks the show, I mean operation is over, and you will have nowhere else to climb but fame's stairwell.

RULE OF FAME # 52:

GET OFF YOUR SOAPBOX AND GET ON A CEREAL BOX

Stop preaching about making it and actually do something that puts you to pitchin' corn or wheat flakes for Kellogg's, Post,—or at least Quaker Oats. If kids are not staring at you each morning, wearing a gold medal around your neck while they are slurping down some sugary puffs, you're losing the fame game. Get on a balance beam, perfect your butterfly stroke, and Mary Lou Rettonize or Michael Phelpsify yourself before it is too late!

Be a media ogre, or be mediocre.

It's the *To be or Not to Be* conundrum of the 21st century.

Stop ranting about the famous and join them.

Do you see the **you** in Youtube? Then **you** post yourself doing something extravagant and sensational. If that talentless high schooler crooning about *It's Friday* can do it, so can you! Discover the victory in going viral, get yourself an aggressive agent, and be the stuff we look at while adding milk and sugar to hydrogenated grains.

Put the General Thrills into General Mills!

And you will have fans and fame for breakfast!

RULE OF FAME # 53: BEWARE THE BRUSH

A brush is not just for unmanageable hair, or worse, unmanageable forest fires. A brush is often what fame will tolerate until it seeks something or someone else it can sink its combed teeth into. Those of you soliciting fame's wares need to look out for the brush. It is the easiest of all items in fame's repertoire to select. It is first, foremost, primary, and most convenient. But...DO NOT PICK UP THAT HOT POTATO. The brush of fame is elusive like a pipe dream, like Barry Sanders darting from a Detroit Lion backfield with, God help him, no blockers. The brush of fame is a mere sampling on a toothpick at Whole Paycheck, I mean Whole Foods. The brush of fame is like that first backpack you run to during the Hungry Games. You pick it up in a frantic fury before a rival tribute plants a meat axe into your lower vertebrae. Unnerving. You scamper off into the woods, unzip it, no not *that*, your backpack—how can you think of doing it at a time like this—unzip your backpack and discover all you have for ammunition is a plastic egg of Silly Putty and a subscription to *Vogue* Well, at least you'll die while looking at world-class models while playing with something soft in your hands.

RULE OF FAME # 54: LIFE IS A CABARET

Do you see the words *cab* and *bar* in *cabaret*? That's right. Take a taxi and trek to the tequila, baby. The pursuit of fame can be rough and edgy. You'll need to smooth those edges by applying shot glasses to your pout like they were your favorite shade of red or pink lipstick. Nothing beats rejection like possessing a show tune in your heart and imported gin in your hand. If you can't shine in the limelight like Evita Peron, you must meander in the smoke and shadows like Sally Bowles played so effortlessly by Judy Garland's daughter, Liza. Someone in that family had to win a competitive acting Oscar!

And you don't need the press as long as you are accompanied and backlit by a mouthy, malicious gay entourage. Bedeck yourself with the boys in the ostrich feathers. If the heels aren't clicking and the brass isn't playing, you're headed for the secretarial pool faster than a stenographer in track cleats. And that is one power walk over lunchtime no one wants to take.

RULE OF FAME # 55: ONE SENIOR MOMENT IN TIME

Like a child born into poverty, you're never too young to fail. Likewise, you are never too old to succeed. It's a whole new twist to the adage, "If at first you don't succeed...wait until you're over the hill when it's all down hill from there." What else are you going to do in your dotage, you useless geezer? Just as you must convince the elderly to adore you, you also must persuade the world to adore you when you are past your prime and about to prune. If you don't believe me, take Betty White, for example. She didn't hit her stride until she played ding-a-ling Rose Nylund on the GOLDEN GIRLS. Now, you can't switch a cable channel without seeing her sagging in a sweat suit on a made-for-LIFETIME movie or TVLand sit com. Ol' Brittle Bones Betty White is making so much money in her 90s, she should change her name to Betty Green.

I plan to do it. How? Well, for starters, I am aging beautifully. Even people who cannot stand me say I look fab-oh for my age. They, on the other hand, look like they went to bed and woke up with a decade smeared all over their face, overnight! You've heard of beauty sleep? Well, this is ugly sleep..and it isn't pretty. Age doesn't always creep and crawl. Sometimes its sprints up on you like the third leg in the men's 4 X 100 relay of the Olympics finale. The next thing you know, you extend your hand to take the baton...only to discover it has more spots than an albino who just lost a black paint gun contest and more wrinkles than fresh linen perpetually caught in a spin cycle.

At this point, friends, you can do one of two things: Get Botox or Get Busy!

I suggest you do the latter and strive for that one senior moment in time of sensationalism before you're called home for good. If Ronald Reagan can run this country while running to the toilet before his Depends drips on the carpet of the Oval Office, you can make something of yourself in your dementia. That's right. Colonel Sandersize yourself and make a name for yourself in those sunset years. Now, the bucket of chicken has already been invented, so that's out. But you know what hasn't? A barrel of ribs!

I bet a barrel of ribs would fly like a plane without terrorists on board! Plus, ribs can stack like Jenga logs. That's bound to have customer appeal! Just flip 'em out of the barrel and pull at 'em one at a time until that tower of ribs comes crumbling down like the World Rib Center. Devastatingly delicious! Change your name to Lieutenant Landers, open a chain of ribs-in-a-barrel stores. And you'd be famous!

Now, I've never been much of a Whitney Houston fan, and I was sorry to read her career literally go down the drain in that bathtub of a Beverly Hills hotel on the eve of the 2012 Grammys, but you've got to admit... that diva could deliver from the belt...and no better than when she demanded "Give me one moment in time." So let me put it in LARGE PRINT FOR YOU OLDIES BUT GOODIES...SEIZURE, I MEAN, SEIZE YOUR ONE SENIOR MOMENT IN TIME! Get restless in that rest home. Retread the *tire* in *retirement*. Tick tock, you old rock. Forget your disastrous past. Believe me, it has fallen and it can't get up, so turn up that hearing aid. FAME IS CALLING!

EPILOGUE

for the truly pathetic still reading this mess

THE TROUBLE WITH TEBOW

AKA, THE TWELVE RANTS OF TEBOW

I.

Tim Tebow's name is an anagram for Mt. Bowtie. And that's about all he is worth, a piece of uncomfortable, ostentatious neckwear. All show and no throw. Speaking of necks, I'd like to strangle his. If he's an NFL quarterback, I am the Queen of Spain who would gladly give him gold to board a ship and discover a new sport to play.

II.

Oh, I can still hear the legions of Tebow devotees defending that lout: *He's all-purpose! He's all-purpose!* Hmmph! All-purpose? So is a sack of flour, but you don't see it strapping on a helmet or kneeling on the sidelines praying to the Sunday afternoon heavens for a better passing rating. But Tim Tebow and a cup of flour do have one thing in common: They both belong in an oven turned up over 450 degrees. Trust me, those cookies, like his career, are done!

III.

I hear he has trademark registered "Tebowing," which is basically getting down on one knee and praying, while specials teams is preparing to kick off and network programming is supposed to break for commercial. "Tebowing" looks like you've got a migraine headache and the only way to rid yourself of it is to get low and flex. He has actually copied Rodin's famous statue, *The Thinker.* But you don't hear any

Parisian artisan yelling, "Copyright infringement." Come to think of it, I wish Tebow were more like statue—made of bronze and marble. Then he'd be able to take a hit without being sidelined like the reserve he was born to be. Please! He couldn't even beat out a Southeast Polk High School alum from Iowa for starting QB in Denver. After being dumped in Denver, the Jets made him a reserve signal caller. If he were still a Jet, I suggest he continue to fly over to Europe and take up soccer.

IV.

But, you have to admit—the guy's on more magazine covers than an address label. You can't stand in line at a grocery store without seeing his mug among the suggest sales of candy bars and lip balm.

V.

O. K. He won a Heisman, but he lost two! After he heisted the Heisman in 2007, Tebow began turning his football career into the downhill skiing exhibition it is today. Alpine Awful. He finished a sorrowful 3rd place in 2008. Then, like a Floridian fool, he stayed for his senior year, only to finish a distant 5th. I mean, some lineman from Nebraska named Ndamukong Suh fared better than Tebow in the 2009 Heisman race. If you're a QB, it helps if you can throw. The only thing Tim Tebow can throw is a fit every time his team loses or God hasn't answered his prayers in a timely fashion. And he can get out of the shot gun and take a backseat to Johnny (Football) Manziel, aka, the Aggie former Freshman sensation from Texas A & M. Tebow is about to find out that everyone and everything is replaceable in hearts and minds of football fans. That's right, Here comes Cocker Manziel. This kid continues to rack up more yards than a card counter in Vegas racks up chips. And he is photogenic, not photohectic.

VI.

Just as Tiny-Talent Tim Tebow has used the NFL as a platform to fame, I intend to use Tebow in this self-yelp book to ascend to the stellar heights of notoriety. I have no other option than to challenge the poor-excuse-for-a-passer to an MMA fight in the off season. That's right, Teetotaler, pull on the trunks and be prepared to be kicked in the face! I'll put your pus back on *GQ: The Black-and-Bruised Edition*.

I hope you have good dental.

VII.

The Jets had Tebow and decided they needed to pass. They needed to pass on Tebow.

VIII.

In a 2012 poll of fellow NFL players, Tim Tebow was named the most overrated player in the game. This, of course, made headlines. Tebow has the fame game coming and going. He possesses the gift of looking good even when he plays like a franchise buster. I myself would have a difficult time ranking his overall football prowess on a scale of 1 to 10, unless you accept fractions. This begs the question: Do NFL passer ratings include negative scores? Perhaps golf is a better way to go for Tebow. Then he could find a sand bunker and dive his head into its trap like an ostrich turning its nest of eggs. At least he'd be off the turf greens and no longer be turning our stomachs.

IX.

Even America's other team, the stinkin', cheatin' New England Patriots don't want him. During the 2013 exhibition season, he was sacked more times than ancient Rome during the pre- and post-Biblical wars. He was sacked more times than the aggregate to-go orders since McDonald's began clogging our nation's archeries, I mean arteries. The

Pats further let him go for an "image" problem he presents for all NFL teams whoever looked at this future poster child for Canadian Football: Tim Tebow is just too famous. He's too popular. So is national debt, but you don't see Congress cutting it like club owners cut Tebow-to-go-go. This, of course, coming from a team that has allegedly filmed more teams without their consent than a sleazy hotel manager with a few too many peepholes in the walls on the first floor. This, of course, coming from a team trying to distance itself from a former tight end with anger management problems But I digress. Tim Tebow is a staple in the American home like salt and sugar, and the "bittersweet" certainly fits him like a girdle on Marilyn Monroe. Too many fans want him to play even if he takes them to the cellar faster than a tornado ripping through the back forty. He is so famous even I have to break my one-page-a-chapter rule in this chintzy book to state his case.

X.

Tebow is the Where's Waldo of the professional sports arena. And quite frankly, I don't give a hit where the hell he is as long as he is not lined up behind the behind of a center of an NFL team I care about.

XI.

But I've got the solution for Tebow and his troubles. Put him on the face of the one-dollar bill instead of Gorgeous George. Yep, the dollar bill. Then at least we'd be able to get four quarters out of him.

XII.

To bum, I mean, sum it all up. Let's face it. Elvis has left the building, and Tim Tebow has left the training facility...again. The last time I heard anything, he was either an analyst or in need of analysis. Either way, he's commenting on plays instead of making them, not exactly the stuff NFL legends are made of.

FEMME FATALE FINALE:

CALL HIM CAITLYN, CALL ME CONFUSED

Lastly, there is a rite of passage to fame, my readers, my peeps. And that passage sails right through the lens for photographer to the stars, Annie Leibovitz. After keeping up with the Kardashians for so long, Bruce, aka, Caitlyn Jenner has surpassed them in a corset-of-courage *Vanity Fair* cover magazine that could give even Alfred Hitchcock the chills! I took one look and began to hum *The Addams Family* theme song. Now, I have to admit that I've only seen the cover. I couldn't bear to look inside. After all, I saw enough flying monkeys hovering around that face that I knew it was best not to enter the witch's castle. And talk about brush ups! Leibovitz gave Ms. Jenner more brushes against that Bedrock body than a hooker receives at a frotteurs' convention.

And what is the purpose to this spread of seven-decade-old margarine across one of our nation's highest of high fashion periodicals? Is Jenner trying to say, *Accept me*.? Because the way he is perched on that godforsaken stool, it looks more like *Do me* or *Take me*. And what's (s)he hiding behind that cinched-to-a-crisp waistline? Man hands!

I have a final confession. I grew up with Bruce. I did. He attended college in my hometown in southern Iowa. I was in grade school. I remember him fondly high hurdling on Tenth Street. He was all stride and thighs back then. Now, (s)he's all string pearls and cramps. And I just don't get it. Is Caitlyn (I think Jennerfer is a better name) trying to express her(m)self? So are lactating mothers breast feeding their young in public parks. I mean, it's hard. (Or is it anymore?) He's gone from

Montreal to Loreal. He was on the cover of my Wheaties box. Now, she's going to illuminate the cover of a Midol box. Give me a minute here, fans. I'm putting my pharmacist on speed dial....there, that's better. There's a sports complex in my hometown named for him. Last time I was there, the floodlights were accessorized with Gucci bags and diva heels. I can't wait for homocoming, I mean, homecoming this fall.

I wish Caitlyn Jenner the best, people, I really do. While others are trying so hard to come out of the closet, she is enjoying her pantie roost by going into a walk-in closet. God knows what waits for her there...the paparazzi, frocks for ex-jocks, and enough shoes to build her a bridge to SanityLand. But I thank the halter bra'ed in an alter ego for letting us all watch when s/he applies all that pancake-pus make-up in his/her waning years just to let Jessica Lange and Susan Lucci know what they're going to look like in 2020. That takes fortitude and a fort of cosmetics. Like Bruce Jenner, I am going out on top. I'm keeping my penis, Adam's apple, and five-o-clock shadow—but I, too, am going out on top. I'm ready for my close-up, Mr. Leibovitz. In closing, is this book or what Miss Jenner is doing all about sensationalism? You tell me, readers. Because when Miss Bruce has her first period, I bet even that, like this book, ends with not so much a period, but an exclamation point!